Dominick Argento

Catalogue Raisonné As Memoir

Catalogue Raisonné As Memoir

A Composer's Life

DOMINICK ARGENTO

University of Minnesota Press
Minneapolis | London

Published by the University of Minnesota Press
111 Third Avenue South, Suite 290
Minneapolis, MN 55401-2520
http://www.upress.umn.edu

Library of Congress Cataloging-in-Publication Data

Argento, Dominick.
Catalogue raisonné as memoir : a composer's life /
Dominick Argento.
p.   cm.
Includes bibliographical references (p.) and index.
ISBN 0-8166-4505-1 (hc : alk. paper)
1. Argento, Dominick. 2. Composers—United
States—Biography. I. Title.
ML410.A687A3 2004
780'.92—dc22

2004006910

Printed in the United States of America on acid-free paper

The University of Minnesota is an equal-opportunity
educator and employer.

12 11 10 09 08 07 06 05 04   10 9 8 7 6 5 4 3 2 1

For Bruce Carlson
with affection, appreciation, and admiration

Greeting.—It is possible that some word of me may have come to you, though even this is doubtful, since an insignificant and obscure name will scarcely penetrate far in either time or space. If, however, you should have heard of me, you may desire to know what manner of man I was, or what was the outcome of my labours, especially those of which some description or, at any rate, the bare titles may have reached you.

—*Francesco Petrarca, Letter to Posterity*

Contents

Preface

∞

I intend this book primarily to furnish
specific data about the music I com-
posed from 1950 to 2002 and, secondarily, to serve as a brief compi-
lation of the places, people, and fugitive thoughts and ideas associated in my mind with those compositions. Remarks about individual
compositions have been kept to roughly one thousand words regard-
less of the work's duration and importance (or lack thereof). At the
outset I had expected that use of the catalogue raisonné form, suggesting a classified and methodical list of artworks, would best accord
with the manner I wished to adopt in presenting this information.
At the beginning of each entry, a block of text gives the essential facts
about each piece. Beneath the title of the composition and the year(s)
it was written is a description of the work's form (or its subtitle) and
its duration in minutes. The next line acknowledges the source of

extramusical components of the composition, if any, and the last lines give the date of the premiere, its location, and the performers or organizations involved.

It soon became apparent that while the classification was simple enough, to write of method (at least in the sense of any regular and systematic procedure followed in composing these pieces) was to attempt articulating the creative process itself, something I have never been able to do to any satisfaction, my own or that of others. Apparently I am not the only composer to have felt stymied or to have offered unenlightening explanations; when asked how he composed, Benjamin Britten replied, "I simply choose a starting note and the rest just naturally follows." While many of my colleagues would grant that Britten's remark corresponds pretty much to their own experience, for the uninitiated that explanation is not particularly illuminating. Consequently, in place of methodology, I am offering a mixed bag of various recollections that account for the appendage of "As Memoir" to the title. These recollections are sometimes about the commissioning of a work and sometimes about its first performance, but only rarely do they address what occurred between those two events—namely, the actual composing of the music.

Strange as it may seem, trying to trace the progression of ideas and thoughts throughout the creative act, at least in my own experience, is virtually impossible. Stranger still: only occasionally does the actual finished work bear a strong resemblance to the work I started to compose, which is to say that most of my compositions, when completed, surprise me by being markedly different from the piece I thought I was composing. While the first few minutes of music are being composed, I feel very much in command of the material and can lead it wherever I wish. But as the composition grows, that control is gradually usurped and the opening material begins to dictate its own continuation, confirming what Britten, succinctly if unhelpfully, referred to as "the rest just naturally follows." My participation now changes to "listening" to the music up to this point and determining where it wants to go or what it wants to do. Dictator becomes amanuensis. Thus the music frequently wants to go places or do things never envisioned in the planning of the piece, resulting in a composition quite unexpected by its composer. These unforeseen outcomes may be great improvements over the original plan or they may be disappointments, in which case they are usually abandoned. To my mind, the clearest analogy is child rearing (a subject about which I know nothing): a parent inculcates ideas, develops tastes, provides guidance, and in effect molds the child from birth through its early years. But the child soon develops its own ideas, cultivates its own tastes, resists external guidance, and ultimately becomes its own master, often with unanticipated results. My compositions, like children, have surprised me that way.

Once a work is completed, the origin of details, the weighing of choices, the constant decision making, false starts, happy surprises, doubts—all these things quickly fade from memory. After enough time has passed, my own compositions become virtually alien to me: I can remember when and where I wrote a piece, but the actual composing, how I wrote it, how I selected this note or this chord to follow that note or that chord, why it does what it does—these are unanswerable questions. Despite my authorship, I have as little knowledge of how a piece of mine was created as I have of the music of strangers. No doubt this must seem an odd situation, but I believe it is readily explained.

Beginning a composition, I feel as though I am entering a separate world, an all-consuming and private world where the usual environment ceases to exist. The mind is concentrated exclusively and intensively on music. Diurnal concerns and problems vanish; meals are missed, appointments forgotten; time assumes a most unclocklike behavior—at times compact, at others highly attenuated. It is an abnormal state of heightened awareness, completely focused on what are, after all, purely arbitrary decisions: Should the next note be higher, lower, or the same? Should it be longer, shorter, or the same? Should it be louder or softer? Should the next chord be more dissonant or less dissonant? Is this section too long or not long enough? Ad infinitum. I speak of these choices as arbitrary because, for the most part, they are not based on reason, principle, or necessity. The composer makes these determinations by instinct because they feel correct or pleasing or inevitable, but logic has played only a small part (if any) in arriving at them. It is impossible to validate this "correctness" or "inevitability" through laws of acoustics or even common sense. The brain's customary role of searching for order and meaning in language and perception has shifted into a more emotion-responding, free-associating, receptive mode, somewhere between semiconsciousness and virtual nonconsciousness. I think this condition is approximately what Leonard Bernstein meant when he said that his first step in composing was to relax to the point of almost falling asleep and allowing the mind to go blank.

When I emerge from a composition session, I feel as if I'm awakening from a trance or an anesthetic. A day or two later, as I make large or small alterations to the completed sections of the music, I view the previous production almost as if it were the work of a different composer. It would seem reasonable to believe that this state of detachment—which grows stronger with the passage of time—would permit the composer to look back over the entire oeuvre and make evaluations with total objectivity and impartiality, but that is not so, at least in my case. Although I recognize that a certain work of mine may be more successful than others with listeners, and a certain work may be more satisfying to me personally than others (and almost never does the same work fit both bills), I hesitate to speak of a favorite work and rarely think of my compositions in that way. The five dozen different pieces catalogued here are just that: pieces, each one of which—from first to last—is part of an extended composition, a single composition that possesses various weaknesses and strengths, naturally, but nevertheless is my musical persona.

This preface has been an attempt (less than successful, I fear) to give the reader some idea of the circumstances and concerns borne in mind while a composer is at work. In the hope of making those abstractions of the compositional process more concrete, I have included at the end of this book portions of the diary I kept during the composition of *The Voyage of Edgar Allan Poe.* It, too, ignores a good deal of technical detail that would not be of general interest and is essentially an emotional barometer of a composer's preoccupations and state of mind during the twenty-two months from conception to completion.

Unsatisfactory as this analysis of the creative process may be, there is also an important corollary that any discussion of music composition must address, one that poses even greater difficulty for this writer: *why* does the composer choose (or invent) and then cultivate a particular musical language, style, manner, or idiom? In all candor, I must admit I don't know. There may be a natural predisposition to go in one direction or another depending on what the composer hopes to accomplish with his music, or perhaps it is partially a question of whether he views his art as essentially emotional or intellectual. Joseph Conrad, in the preface to *The Nigger of the "Narcissus,"* states his position—one with which I fully concur—as follows: "The artist descends within himself, and in that lonely region of stress and strife, if he be deserving and fortunate, he finds the terms of his appeal . . . he appeals to that part of our being which is not dependent on wisdom, to that in us which is a gift and not an acquisition . . . such an appeal, to be effective, must be an impression conveyed through the senses . . . it is not amenable to persuasion . . . *its high desire is to reach the secret springs of responsive emotion*" (my emphasis).

In compiling the table of contents, I became aware of a particular I hadn't noticed before: there are virtually no examples of abstract music. With the exception of *String Quartet* (which remains in manuscript), *Capriccio for Clarinet and Orchestra* (which is somewhat programmatic), and *Divertimento for Piano and Strings,* there are no sonatas, no symphonies, no concertos. In spite of the university position I happily filled for forty years, I managed to avoid its major occupational hazard: becoming an academic composer, with all the unattractive connotations that title holds. The affective content of my music seems to depend less on intrinsic form than on some narrative element, the latter usually manifesting itself as storytelling. And that is odd, because my focus, at the outset, was essentially on instrumental composition, primarily music for piano and rarely music employing a text or singers. By the time my education was completed, ten years later, my interests had taken an entirely different direction.

What accounts for so marked a change of focus? More than one writer has observed that the theme of self-discovery permeates my operas and, to a lesser extent, the song cycles: *gnothi seauton,* know thyself. At the beginning, I was totally unaware of this predilection: without asking myself why, I have always been drawn to stories or situations that deal with a character learning something about himself that significantly changes his life—shades of Oedipus. This action is treated comically (in *The Boor*), seriously (in *The Aspern Papers*), lightheartedly (in *Casanova's Homecoming*), historically (in *The Andrée Expedition*), fantastically (in *The Voyage of Edgar Allan Poe*), surrealistically (in *Postcard from Morocco*), and even religiously (in *Jonah and the Whale*), but it is ever present. So I suppose my shift in focus might be regarded as a case of life mimicking art, because that early decade of writing music—mostly music later discarded—also imitated that same action, which is to say it was a way of learning something about myself, and with that self-knowledge my outlook was changed.

Songs about Spring
(1950)

∞

Three songs for soprano and piano (two were added in 1955;
    all five were orchestrated in 1960)
12 minutes
Poetry by e e cummings
Piano version performed 22 May 1951, Peabody Conservatory,
    Baltimore, Maryland; Carolyn Bailey, soprano; Dominick
    Argento, piano
Orchestral version performed 14 July 1960, Eastman School of
    Music, Rochester, New York; Carolyn Bailey, soprano;
    Frederick Fennell, conductor, Kilbourn Hall Orchestra

I began to compose around the time of
the attack on Pearl Harbor, which is to
say between my fourteenth and fifteenth birthdays, although *Songs about
Spring,* which I consider my opus 1, was not written until I was almost
twenty-three years old. Songs 1, 2, and 3 were composed in the summer of 1950 at the Cummington School of the Arts in Massachusetts,
where Hugo Weisgall, a staff member, had obtained a scholarship for
me. Hugo was not on the faculty of the Peabody Conservatory, where
I was enrolled at the time, but he was the best-known composer in
Baltimore, and we had met earlier that year at a party following the
performance of one of his works. We had only a brief conversation
and for some reason he took an interest in me. That summer he was
working on his first opera, *The Tenor,* and he played its newly composed
pages for me each afternoon after our lesson on my songs.

Of all the music I composed in my undergraduate years at Peabody (1947–51)—*String Trio* and *Piano Sonata,* three short choruses on texts by Rabindranath Tagore, some minor orchestral pieces—only *Songs about Spring* remains, which is to say that everything composed while I studied under Nicholas Nabokov (my primary teacher at the conservatory) was later destroyed. Looking back, I realize that Nicky was a poor teacher and taught me virtually nothing about composition. I chose to study with him because I was awed by the fact that he was a close friend of Stravinsky's (always referred to as "Igor Fyodorovich"), and, like Stravinsky himself, he had at one time been an intimate of the great Russian impresario Sergei Diaghilev and was acquainted with many of the artists in his circle: Nijinsky, Ravel, Prokofiev, Picasso, and others. Diaghilev had commissioned Nabokov to compose a work for his Paris-based Les Ballets Russes. Titled *Ode, or Meditation on the Aurora Borealis,* it was given a sumptuous production but failed.

Often unprepared for my Monday one-hour lessons at 3 p.m., Nicky would invite me across Mount Vernon Place, past the tall tower surmounted by a statue of George Washington, to the University Club, where I learned to drink martinis and listened to stories about the weekend he had just spent with Stravinsky in California. Sometimes at my lessons he would show me the latest pages of Stravinsky's manuscript of *The Rake's Progress,* which he was conveying to the music publisher, Boosey & Hawkes, in New York City, where he resided part of the week. He was not a particularly successful composer, though I remember a fine piece for mezzo and orchestra (commissioned by Serge Koussevitsky, then conductor of the Boston Symphony) whose premiere Nicky conducted while not entirely sober. The poem for that work, "The Return of Pushkin," had been translated into English by his cousin Vladimir in his pre-*Lolita* days. Nicky also worked part-time in Washington for the Voice of America during the hunt for Reds. He said his most significant contribution was unmasking the radio theme song for *The FBI in Peace and War* as the work of a Communist (the march from Prokofiev's *Love for Three Oranges*).

Nicky encouraged me to apply for a Fulbright to study in Florence—a life-altering experience. I was awarded the grant and spent the year, along with four fellow Fulbrighters, in a splendid villa we rented at via San Leonardo 72, not far from the Piazzale Michelangelo. I was charmed by the names of the couple in charge: the housekeeper-cook was Domenica; her husband, the gardener-caretaker, was Domenico. (A few years later, Hugo and his family—thanks to a Guggenheim grant and upon my recommendation—rented the same villa where he began work on his masterpiece, *Six Characters in Search of an Author*.)

When I left for Florence, Nabokov departed for Paris and Berlin to run an international arts festival later exposed as a front for the CIA. He gave me his address in France and encouraged me to write to him with news of my progress. I wrote to him (around Christmas, 1951), and since my lessons had not been going well—my teacher was the latest darling of the twelve-tone music set and was pushing me in a direction I found repugnant at the time—I made a foolish remark comparing the recently deceased Arnold Schoenberg and Savonarola, the fifteenth-century religious reformer. I thought my comments would be ingratiating since at that time the Stravinsky-Schoenberg rivalry split virtually all composers into two camps, and Stravinsky had no greater proponent than Nicky. Evidently finding my humor offensive, he never replied to that letter and I never heard from him again. (I still find a surprising affinity between the firebrand monk and the father of serialism: the fierce glower one sees in photographs of Schoenberg and in portraits of Savonarola are perfectly interchangeable.) Being in New York in 1975 and with his finger always on the pulse of new music, Nicky had to have known that I won the Pulitzer Prize, but not a word came from him.

Nonetheless, I always remember him fondly as an extraordinary man: he was the only genuine cosmopolite I have ever known, spoke half a dozen languages fluently, married five beautiful women (the last was an editor at *Vogue*), was acquainted with every important living artist in Europe and America, authored two semiautobiographical books about contemporary music, and encouraged one uncertain freshman piano major to switch to a major in composition, for which I will be eternally grateful. A photograph taken in 1971, at the funeral service held for Stravinsky in the basilica of Venice's San Marco, shows Nabokov occupying the center seat of the front row, a tall, distinguished, white-haired figure serving as a firewall between the hostile factions of Stravinsky's first and second families.

For my senior recital (a program of original works) I needed a soprano to perform *Songs about Spring*. I consulted Peter DeLone, a student composer like myself and my best friend, who was surprised that I didn't know about the terrific soprano from my own hometown of York, Pennsylvania. Her name was Carolyn Bailey, and at the age of fifteen she had been given a personal scholarship by one of Peabody's principal voice teachers and became a conservatory matriculate in 1948. Despite the fact that we must have shared the same Greyhound or train many weekends during the fifty-mile trip back and forth between Baltimore and York, we had never met. A blind date was soon arranged, and over dessert I revealed my ulterior motive. Yes, of course, she'd be happy to sing the cycle. So at the recital, Carolyn gave the premiere performance of these songs and I was the accompanist, a role I played for a number of her recitals later on. What I did not know at the time was that for many years to come she would sing the premiere of everything I composed for soprano and serve as an invaluable adviser on matters vocal; best of all, I would remain her accompanist in another sense: three years later she became my wife.

Sicilian Limes
(1953)

∾

Opera in one act
55 minutes
Libretto by John Olon-Scrymgeour, based on the play by Luigi
    Pirandello
Performed 14 April 1954, Peabody Conservatory, Baltimore,
    Maryland; Malcolm Bernstein, baritone; Lorraine Panek,
    mezzo; Carolyn Bailey, soprano; et al. John Hutton and
    Dominick Argento, pianists; Hugo Weisgall, director and
    conductor

After completing my bachelor's degree, I wrote *The Temptation of Saint Joseph* (oratorio on W. H. Auden, completed in Florence in 1951) and *Aria Da Capo* (one-act opera on Edna St. Vincent Millay, only two-thirds finished later during that same Fulbright year—its completion was discouraged by Hugo). It had been Nabokov's recommendation that I study with Luigi Dallapiccola, Italy's most successful contemporary composer, whose reputation had become international in the preceding decade. In Florence I showed the oratorio and *Songs about Spring* to Dallapiccola, who strongly disapproved of my harmonic sense and started me at basics, a single line setting of a Latin text. The language was chosen as neutral ground: he spoke very little English and I knew very little Italian. He faulted my assignments for repeating certain notes too often, and I realized I was being nudged toward dodecaphony.

(Twelve-tone music—in which any given note is not to be repeated until the other eleven have been presented—after being relatively dormant during the quarter century following its invention, was spreading rapidly after World War II.) Serialism, another name for the technique, was anathema to me at the time. Dallapiccola's opera, *Il prigioniero,* written in that system, had had a fine success at Tanglewood, where he had been a guest teacher the previous summer (were classes held in Latin? I wonder). Nevertheless, I resisted being pushed in that direction, and after three or four lessons I stopped making the long trek out to his home in via Bolognese and never saw him again. Years later, when I matured a bit more, I made my accommodation with serialism, and, oddly enough, it was Dallapiccola's brand—Italianate and vaguely tonal—not Schoenberg's, that I chose to emulate.

Sicilian Limes was composed the year and two summers I worked on my master's degree at Peabody, studying under Henry Cowell. Henry was a kindly, small man with a bushy fringe of white hair surrounding a knobby bald pate: he looked like nothing so much as an impish friar or a leprechaun, belying his reputation as one of twentieth-century music's most noted mavericks. If one could believe Henry, my first opera was easily the equal to *Don Giovanni:* everything I showed him was just fine, wonderful. I was fully aware that his reluctance to be critical was the result of a prison sentence—1936 to 1940—he had served in San Francisco on charges of homosexuality. Even fifteen years after parole he had not lost the prison mark. It made him pathetically fearful of offending anyone.

Pete DeLone and I invited him to Pete's apartment for an evening. Over after-dinner drinks we urged him to perform some of his experimental piano pieces. He happily obliged, removing the front of Pete's century-old, rented upright in order to attack the strings directly: the handle of a soup spoon in his left hand forcefully rasping the lowest strings and his right elbow smashing out cluster chords at the upper end of the keyboard. He suddenly interrupted himself, brightened, and told us of a review he received after the

German premiere of his *Piano Concerto* (in which he was the soloist) sometime in the 1920s, one of the earliest works to use cluster
chords: "Vy does Herr Cowell use his forearm ven he could cover
many more notes vit his behind?" Great clouds of ancient gray dust
billowed out of the instrument as Henry continued his performance,
but he seemed oblivious to them. By the end of the evening, arms,
head, and shoulders thickly encrusted with dust, he resembled a statue
in the park that had been the residence for many pigeons.

Shortly after its premiere at Peabody (with two pianos instead of orchestra), whatever future *Sicilian Limes* might have had was
quickly blighted: a brief item in the *New York Times* announcing that
the After Dinner Opera Company (a chamber opera group in that
city) planned a performance of it in the fall drew the attention of
the Pirandello Estate to my failure to obtain their permission. There
was no question of a student being able to afford the rights, so the
opera was withdrawn. (A few years later, Hugo Weisgall purchased
rights from the estate for *Six Characters in Search of an Author* at a cost of
$7,500, which no doubt was as much as or more than the commis-
sioning fee he received to compose the opera.) Almost four decades
later, out of sheer curiosity (but primarily because the copyright had
now expired), I allowed a revival of *Sicilian Limes* by the University of
Minnesota's opera department and heard it for the only time with
orchestra. It was like hearing the music of a stranger: none of the
thrill and excitement I had felt at that first performance with two
pianos was repeated in the revival when what I felt was mostly sympathy for the young and unsure composer trying his hardest to cope.
It's certainly not too bad for a first effort, although Hugo complained
(incorrectly, I still think) that there was far too much Aunt Marta
music—he regarded her as the least significant of the three leading
characters. I, on the other hand, found her pivotal. Carolyn sang
the role of Teresina, the plot's opera diva, performing from behind the scenery because an interesting dramaturgical conceit had
it that, among friends and admirers at the offstage party, she sings

beautifully, but when she appears onstage, to confront her erstwhile boyfriend, Teresina (now played by an actress) addresses him icily in plain speech.

The opera remains withdrawn. As long ago as 1770, the composer Christoph Willibald Gluck said that first operas, like first litters, ought to be mercifully drowned and with very few exceptions—only Monteverdi's *Orfeo* and Alban Berg's *Wozzeck* come to mind—that still seems to be sound advice. Little did I think at the time that *Sicilian Limes* would have a dozen successors or that I would end up known primarily as a composer of opera. Certainly the acquaintance with Hugo at this stage of my life was decisive. Prior to hearing his own opera and his introducing me to the operas of Benjamin Britten, the form had no appeal for me. People often assume that my interest in opera must stem from an Italian heritage, but in fact it is due, oddly enough, to the influence of an American and an Englishman—nationalities not renowned for their operatic tradition. On the other hand, perhaps it is not so strange since, in my opinion, both men were the finest opera composers their nations had ever produced.

Divertimento for
Piano and Strings
(1954)

∞

17 minutes
Performed 11 July 1956, Eastman School of Music, Rochester,
New York; Richard Woitach, piano; Frederick Fennell,
conductor, Kilbourn Hall Orchestra

Divertimento for Piano and Strings was written during the first year of our marriage and the third and final year of my first academic appointment, at Hampton Institute in Virginia, a college founded in 1868 to educate newly freed slaves. The work was strongly influenced by Ernst Bloch's *Concerto Grosso no. 2 for Piano and Strings.* Carolyn particularly liked the Bloch and we frequently played the recording. *Divertimento* was my first piece of music publicly performed in Minneapolis, by Tom Nee conducting the Unitarian Society Orchestra in 1959. At intermission (just before the performance of the work) the *Minneapolis Star*'s music critic, to prove that he was au courant, asked me if the piece was going to be twelve-tone. No, I said, on the contrary, it was very much a celebration of C major. (I had originally planned to title it *Landscape with Figures,* an homage to such favorite composers as Weber, Mendelssohn, and Grieg, whose music I had learned to love through my piano lessons.) The next day in his critique the reviewer insisted *Divertimento* was an atonal work. It was my first personal brush with that most inexact of sciences, music criticism.

While at Hampton, in addition to the *Divertimento,* I set to music two more e e cummings poems to be added to the *Songs about Spring* cycle, and an abridged version of the oratorio *The Temptation of Saint Joseph* (still unorchestrated) was premiered with piano accompaniment. Realizing that some of Dallapiccola's criticism of the piece had merit, I subsequently withdrew it. A good deal of time was spent considering two other projects that never came to anything: an opera based on Lorca's *Doña Rosita* and a ballet on Hawthorne's *The Scarlet Letter.* Classes and private lessons consumed a great deal of my time, and one of my favorite teaching anecdotes comes from this period. An elderly black gentleman in his midsixties who worked as a chef for a hotel in nearby Old Point Comfort phoned and told me he heard music in his head and wanted to learn how to write it down. His lesson time was set for 3:30 p.m. (between the lunch and dinner rushes), and he arrived in his kitchen costume, hat included, redolent of culinary pleasures. Since he was musically illiterate, I started him with rudiments of rhythmic notation and, at the blackboard, showed him how to draw half notes (stem and empty notehead), quarter notes (stem and filled-in notehead), and so forth, and explained their worth. I gave him a homework exercise consisting of blank measures in different time signatures to be accurately completed using a mixture of these various values. He assured me he understood, but the next week his completed assignment proved otherwise: his half notes were quarters and his quarters were halves. I began to reexplain, but he interrupted: "Well, look here, Mr. Argento," he said, pointing at the blackboard, "last week your halfs had black middles and your quarters had white ones. That's just what mine got on this here paper." Race was a crucial distinguishing element at Hampton, and even the music notes were seen by this student solely in terms of color, black vs. white.

When the school year ended Carolyn and I took positions as counselors at Camp Tapawingo, a New England summer camp for Jewish girls—jobs that Hugo obtained for us. As music director I gave piano lessons, prepared the performance of a musical (*Oklahoma)*, and began work on another opera (John Olon-Scrymgeour's libretto of the Alfred de Musset play *Fantasio*). Earlier that year I had decided to apply to the Eastman School of Music and had received a dual scholarship as opera coach and theory teaching fellow. Carolyn studied voice and was accepted into the opera department. I still recall entering Eastman that first day of classes very apprehensive because of my poor preparation at Peabody. I carried a folded-up copy of the *New York Times* under my arm to demonstrate my sophistication. It took a number of weeks before I no longer felt out of my element.

Despite Hugo's flattering and oft-repeated statement of how much he envied my technical skill in composition and orchestration, I have always felt far less than confident, even insecure. In truth, I cannot say that I learned much very about composition from most of the seven composers under whom I studied—and a very mixed bag they were: Nabokov, Weisgall, Dallapiccola, Cowell, and now at Eastman, Bernard Rogers (the finest teacher of them all), Alan Hovhaness (the most original composer among my teachers), and Howard Hanson (the director of the school and a distinguished composer himself). What I did learn came mostly from knowing them and their music, not from actual lessons. I was to discover that the same could be said of me when I became a teacher: I imparted precious few pearls of wisdom. And although I realized that students tend to emulate the teachers with whom they study, I tried not to allow that to influence their natural inclinations. Michelangelo's theory about simply chipping away the excess marble until the figure locked inside was revealed seemed equally applicable to the teaching of composition: most of my criticisms were negative—subtraction rather than addition—and directed at a student's bad habits, slipshod work, unfulfilled ideas, easy solutions: in short, developing musical character rather than molding musical style.

When I first entered Peabody I had wanted to become one of those pianist-composers who specialize in their own music, like Chopin, Liszt, Rachmaninoff, Prokofiev, Gershwin. But early in that first year at Peabody it became apparent that I would never make it as a pianist—beginning lessons at the advanced age of sixteen left me too far behind the other students. However, I astonished Nabokov by breezing through all four years of harmony in those first nine months. (Even before starting piano lessons, I had begun to teach myself theory and instrumentation through books borrowed from the public library because they seemed necessary adjuncts to the career I had in mind.) Nicky asked if I composed. Mostly piano pieces, I told him. He then gave me the oddest advice: over the summer I should compose more instrumental pieces and read the letters of Mozart. That was Nabokov's gift to me. When I returned for my sophomore year I changed my major and won the annual composition prize.

From Weisgall, the gift was the discovery that vocal music—operatic, choral, song, combining a love of literature and music—was my natural musical home. From Dallapiccola, the example of how to bend an uncongenial technique of composition to serve one's own purposes. From Rogers, an abiding respect, even reverence, for artistic integrity: no shortcuts, never settle for anything less than the best you have. From Hovhaness, the importance of spontaneity and going one's own way, fashionable or not. From Cowell and Hanson, that kindness and generosity can sometimes be more valuable to a young composer than criticism and advice.

The Resurrection of Don Juan
(1955)

∾

Ballet, 45 minutes
Suite for orchestra, 22 minutes
Scenario by Richard Hart
Ballet suite performed 5 May 1956, Festival of American Music,
    Eastman School of Music, Rochester, New York
Complete ballet performed winter 1959, Staatstheater, Karlsruhe,
    West Germany

My first composition lesson with Bernard Rogers at Eastman could not have been more devastating, particularly since my self-esteem was at its nadir. When I showed him a trio and some other finished bits of *Fantasio* he was mightily unimpressed, criticizing my text setting and the subject in general as hopeless. I abandoned the opera and decided to try a different work for the stage, one without text: a ballet, *The Resurrection of Don Juan,* to an ingenious scenario by Richard Hart, a poet and head of the Enoch Pratt Library in Baltimore. To my surprise, Rogers praised the finished score (written in four or five weeks) and, evidently forgetting that he had panned my operatic excerpts earlier, said I seemed to have a flair for the stage. Had I ever considered composing an opera? Still smarting from his criticism of *Fantasio,* I lied, saying no.

A suite from the ballet was sight-read with orchestra that spring at the composers' symposium (one of three dozen or more student works) and created a real stir among both fellow students and faculty. Howard Hanson, the school's director, selected it as the only student piece programmed on his annual Festival of American Music a few weeks later. (The complete ballet was produced in West Germany several years thereafter; I never saw anything of it except for some photographs and positive reviews. The ballet suite has the distinction of being the first piece of mine played by the then Minneapolis Symphony, under Tom Nee, in a program of music by University of Minnesota faculty composers.) When Hanson performed the suite at the festival, it was the first orchestral score of mine I ever really heard well played and I will confess it dazzled me. I could scarcely believe that I was responsible for those bright sonorities and fascinating colors emerging from that orchestra: the experience was exhilarating beyond words.

Composition is sometimes a struggle, but orchestration (as far as the one can be separated from the other) is always an enjoyable and easy task, even though it is tedious, eyestraining labor writing down the thousands and thousands of notes required, sometimes for a passage lasting less than a minute. Yet it never fails to thrill me when a combination of sounds I've dryly worked out in silence on paper is finally performed by instruments: it reminds me of those childhood experiments—usually guesswork—I used to indulge in with a toy chemistry set, hoping to create invisible ink, secret poisons, or gunpowder. Those results were almost always disappointing or outright failures, unlike orchestration, where the effect is frequently a happy surprise and, more often than not, much finer than anything I expected.

A few years earlier, at Peabody, *Sicilian Limes* had been scheduled to be done with the school orchestra, but it was canceled after a single rehearsal because the conductor, George Hurst, said he needed much more time with the orchestra to prepare his all-Beethoven program.

We were forced to use two pianos instead. Until 1956, the only actual performance of an orchestral work of mine had been *Introduction and Allegro,* which the York (Pennsylvania) Symphony had commissioned and then performed abominably under the same George Hurst, whose position with my hometown orchestra I had helped him obtain. Nabokov, who was still my teacher at the time (1951), came up to York from Baltimore for the performance, which I am sure he did not enjoy nearly as much as my father's homemade wine at the post-performance party. His opinion (of my music, not the wine): it's a fine *green* piece. Yet even in that poorly played piece of juvenilia, there were a few moments of unanticipated orchestral effects that sent an electrical jolt through me.

During the summer between my two academic years at Eastman, I studied with Alan Hovhaness, whose reputation was fast increasing during that period. His second symphony, *Mysterious Mountain,* became one of the most frequently programmed works for a number of seasons. Alan was a very gentle but sickly man. When I arrived for my first lesson I watched him for about five minutes through the window in the classroom door before entering: he was lunching on canned baby food and melted ice cream; blank manuscript paper covered every available flat surface—the piano top, desktops, seats of chairs, windowsills. As he ate, he wandered erratically about the room, writing a few notes on one page, then crossing the room to write a few more notes on a different page, more notes on the pages on his desk, and so on. He gave the impression of a tall, lean butterfly pollinating a field of flowers. I was fascinated and mystified. Later he explained his method of composing. Rarely working as most composers do—starting with a beginning and continuing straight on through to an end—he preferred to work on disjunct sections at the same time, where an idea he was jotting down on one page would suggest something he could use in a passage that might come much later (or earlier) in the piece. He was by far the most spontaneous and prolific composer I ever knew. At Eastman he showed me the score of his recently completed setting of Saint-John Perse's *Anabasis*. It was at least three inches thick.

Around the time Hovhaness reached middle age, he destroyed all his earlier music—and there was a tremendous quantity of it—to begin anew in that hypnotic Armenian style for which he is now best remembered. I saw him for the last time many years later in Minneapolis, when Carolyn and I took him and his lovely wife to dinner before the premiere by the Minnesota Orchestra of a new work of his—I believe it was *Concerto for Euphonium*—whose opus number was already well into the hundreds.

Ode to the West Wind
(1956)

∾

Concerto for soprano and orchestra
28 minutes
Poetry by Percy Bysshe Shelley
Performed 29 April 1957, Festival of American Music, Eastman
    School of Music, Rochester, New York; Carolyn Bailey,
    soprano; Howard Hanson, conductor, Eastman-Rochester
    Philharmonic

B ernard Rogers thought my ballet revealed not only a gift for dramatic music but a lyric gift as well: had I done much text setting? He made the odd suggestion that I consider taking a crack at Shelley's "Ode to the West Wind," adding that, given the poem's greatness, he himself had never had the nerve to tackle it and doubted whether I'd be able to do much justice to the text either. Still, if I cared to try . . . I did not tell him that Shelley's verse was the reason I got a D in undergraduate English lit at Johns Hopkins: the final exam asked us to discuss at length what the poet was saying. I had been spending all my time outside of class composing music and hadn't even read the poem, nor had I received much illumination from the professor's post-martini exegesis (academic courses were held after the dinner hour for Peabody students). A year later, in Florence, I learned that

Shelley composed the work seated on the banks of the Arno, and now I found it particularly interesting.

When I finished the score Bernard was impressed and said, "Okay. There's your Ph.D. thesis. Now what do you want to write?" Neither of us had assumed at the outset that it would take such a form. It was too late to copy parts for the symposium that first year, since I was still copying parts for the ballet, so it had to wait until the following year, when Carolyn performed it magnificently at both the symposium and the festival. On the day of the festival performance, being nervous, she practiced a good part of the day and sang the whole thing through just before the concert, leaving us both concerned that she might not have enough voice left for the actual performance. We needn't have worried. She gave a truly glorious account of the piece, and later, when Hanson finished playing the tape of their performance for my Ph.D. oral examination committee, he declared that Carolyn ought to receive a degree of some sort as well for her wonderful rendition, perhaps a Ph.T.—Putting hubby Through.

Having entered Eastman almost apologetically, sure that I was outclassed by every other composition student in the school, by the end of that first year I had the distinct feeling that there was an invisible laurel wreath on my head. Bernard was primarily responsible for this change of attitude. I was very downhearted at my first lesson when he casually dismissed the fragments of *Fantasio* as hopeless (rightly so, as I later understood), but little by little I warmed to him and he to me. After a couple of months he invited Carolyn and me to spend an evening at his home. These visits soon became weekly events and a fast friendship developed between us. Even though I had my studies with Hanson in my second Eastman year, our socializing with Bernard continued up through and beyond graduation. He warned me not to take the teaching job at Eastman that Hanson would surely offer me: he felt that remaining in Hanson's shadow had blighted his own career and would do the same for me. I did go back to teach at Eastman for several summers after I accepted my position in Minnesota, mainly to spend those six weeks with Bernard, but when Hanson offered me a full-time appointment, I said no.

My two favorites of the seven composers with whom I studied, men I truly loved and was most influenced by, were both unfortunate victims of a hostile press. Although he never attained the appreciation and respect he deserved (I still regard his *Six Characters in Search of an Author* of 1959—despite opening to mixed reviews and disappearing shortly thereafter—as the finest opera ever produced in this country), Hugo Weisgall somehow survived a lifetime of critical abuse, of neglect, and continued blithely on his chosen path until, in his eighties, he finally had one unequivocal triumph with the New York City Opera's premiere of *Esther,* a work originally commissioned by San Francisco Opera and then rejected. Its great success with audience and press was sufficient to occasion a revival in a subsequent season, but before it could take place, Hugo died. The planned revival was quietly shelved—*sic transit gloria mundi.*

Bernard's career, on the contrary, was virtually ruined thanks to a single review. His opera *The Warrior,* a setting of Norman Corwin's radio drama about Samson and Delilah, won a contest sponsored by the Metropolitan around 1945. Its single performance—a New Year's Day matinee at the Met (double-billed with, of all things, *Hansel and Gretel*)—was ridiculed by New York's most powerful critic, Olin Downes. Unable to vent his spleen fully in his long Sunday column, Downes continued to savage the opera on the following Sunday. His terrible outrage still unappeased—once more on a third Sunday: the nastiest and most vicious case of critical overkill I ever heard of. Prior to the premiere, a studio portrait of Bernard appeared in *Vogue* in an article about the contest. It shows the man's strong face, firm and confident, secure in himself. The teacher I met a decade after the Downes review had the much softer face of a broken, defeated man.

String Quartet
(1956)

∾

20 minutes
Performed 17 January 1957, Kilbourn Hall, Eastman School
of Music, Rochester, New York; student performers

String Quartet no. 1 (it has remained singular) was composed in the summer
between my first and second years at Eastman when I studied with
Alan Hovhaness. Composition was surely as much Alan's natural
element as water is to a fish. I mentioned earlier that he was an extremely prolific composer, writing music effortlessly and rapidly. I,
too, was a relatively fast composer, but his example inspired me to try
writing more spontaneously; as Verdi said, "Art without spontaneity
is stillborn." I chose one of my favorite Mozart quartets, studied
and analyzed a single movement each morning, then composed one
of my own in the afternoon, a movement a day. A day or two for
revisions and making a fair copy, and the piece was finished in less
than a week, on time for my second lesson. At my first lesson I had
merely shown Alan some pieces I had composed earlier: *Don Juan, Ode,*

and *Divertimento.* He praised them all but was particularly partial to *Divertimento,* no doubt because, of those three works, it seemed to him to be (and was) the most spontaneously composed piece. He immediately wrote a note to the school's conductor, Frederick Fennell, urging its performance on one of Fred's summer concerts. I still have the note ("This is important!!") written in Alan's distinctive scrawl, with letters two and three inches high and triply underscored.

After the successful completion of that first Eastman year—I had composed a forty-five-minute ballet and a thirty-minute soprano/orchestra work, despite a daily teaching load and many hours accompanying opera workshop, in addition to the full number of degree courses I was required to take—my self-esteem had been strengthened considerably. It was apparent that I had become Rogers's favorite pupil; Hanson's inclusion of the *Don Juan* suite in his festival had been an unexpected honor; and now the good impression I seemed to have made on Hovhaness added to my confidence.

The contrast between Rogers and Hovhaness could not have been more striking. Music simply poured out of Alan, and I'm sure he rarely was bothered by second thoughts or spent much time revising or improving a piece. I intend nothing negative by that observation, for that most certainly must have been the way of Mozart, Bach, Vivaldi, and many others. But for Bernard the model would have been a composer more like Beethoven—painfully meticulous, always questioning the slightest detail, frequently dissatisfied, not only with his own music but with most of the work of his students. *Ode to the West Wind* had been composed in a few months, and although Bernard liked much of it, he found the closing pages of the piece to be a real letdown and insisted that I had to find something at least a shade closer to the magnificent optimism of Shelley's lines concluding with "If Winter comes, can Spring be far behind?" Failing that, he said, there was no point in composing the piece at all. He admitted that when he had once considered setting Shelley's poem, it was that challenge that made him hold back.

Even though I thought my original ending was the best I could do, for the next couple of weeks I reworked the final pages over and over, but nothing pleased him and my feelings were very hurt when he commented that it may have been a mistake to suggest that I tackle the Shelley text. Goaded, I tried several more times. Finally Bernard was satisfied with everything but the final chord. He said it was simply not "radiant" enough: the concluding sonority had to encapsulate the preceding half hour, to bring everything together in one joyous noise—*finis coronat opus*. At my next lesson I complained that I had tried every conceivable combination of three, four, five, and six notes, but nothing seemed to do the trick. With a voice dripping sarcasm Bernard said, "Did you know there are over a million and a half combinations possible on a piano keyboard using only three notes: imagine the astronomical number when one, two, or three more notes are thrown into the mix. Are you *sure* you tried them all?" Back to the drawing board. When I returned with what I hoped would be acceptable to him, he listened, smiled, nodded his head, and said, "That's it."

The Boor
(1957)

∾

Opera buffa in one act
55 minutes
Libretto by John Olon-Scrymgeour, based on the play by
    Anton Chekhov
Performed 6 May 1957, Festival of American Music, Eastman
    School of Music, Rochester, New York; Robert Duval,
    baritone; Barbara Altman, soprano; Nicholas DiVirgilio,
    tenor; Frederick Fennell, conductor, Kilbourn Hall
    Orchestra

The Boor was the major work written during my second year at Eastman while studying under Howard Hanson, as was required of all second-year composition Ph.D.'s. The opera had emerged with surprising ease, and I don't recall a single criticism made by Hanson as I showed him the weekly installments. When it was finished he said he would like to have the opera presented during the annual festival. I pointed out that he had already told Bernard Rogers (who had shown him the score the previous year) that he was going to schedule *Ode to the West Wind* on that year's festival. I still had those parts to prepare for the upcoming symposium; there simply was not enough time for me also to copy parts for an hour-long opera. He told me to turn the score over to Litch Tolland, the calligraphy teacher and professional copyist. The school would pay for the copying, which certainly must have exceeded a thousand dollars. I was astonished.

The Boor, programmed on a double bill with Bernard's The Nightingale, was a rousing success. Fred Fennell conducted it and notified music publishers Boosey & Hawkes, Schirmer, and Galaxy of its reception. All three asked me to send a tape recording and to come to New York for an interview. I arranged to visit each one in a single day a few weeks later. In the morning I visited Hans Heinsheimer at Schirmer, who very offhandedly announced that he hadn't had time to listen to the recording yet. His office was cluttered with proofs, parts, and scores of Samuel Barber's new opera, Anthony and Cleopatra, commissioned for the opening of the Met at Lincoln Center, the musical event of the year. He promised to listen to my tape when he was less busy, but until then I shouldn't accept any other offer. That was particularly annoying since he had had the score and recording for weeks and knew I was coming to New York that day to see him. Robert Ward, himself a noted composer of opera who worked for Galaxy Publications, took me to lunch and said he would love to publish The Boor but felt that if Boosey or Schirmer offered to take it, they could do far more for me than his small company. In the afternoon, when I went to Boosey, they already had a contract waiting for me. Word eventually must have reached Heinsheimer that I had signed with Boosey because a few weeks later I received a package from him. There was no note: only my score and several hundred feet of recording tape crushed up in its box. Years later I ran across Heinsheimer, who was by then doing promotional work for Boosey, but he never acknowledged our previous meeting.

The Boor, I believe, was a vast improvement over my earlier opera owing to the coaching I was doing at the time in the Eastman opera department. I'd had some experience earlier as music director and coach in Baltimore between the time I finished my bachelor's degree and completed the master's. Hugo Weisgall had organized a modest summer-stock kind of company (we played in an old barn in the

Maryland countryside) called the Hilltop Opera. We specialized in contemporary operas—Milhaud, Hindemith, Britten, two of Hugo's own pieces (*The Tenor* and *The Stronger*), and some other Americans—although we also did *The Mikado* and *The Bartered Bride.* Hugo staged and conducted everything. Exposure to the works we performed that first season made me see the potential that opera offered a composer. Before this experience, which I undertook only because it provided some income, I was mainly (but poorly) acquainted with nineteenth-century opera and considered it a moribund and frivolous form of music. During my Fulbright year in Florence I had begun to compose (and completed much of) *Aria Da Capo,* which might have been my first opera had Hugo not pointed out its weaknesses. The following year, with still more experience and under the sympathetic eye of Henry Cowell, I started—and this time completed—another opera on a much worthier dramatic subject: *Sicilian Limes.* I was now addicted to the opera form.

Two or three months before school ended, I received by mail—unsolicited—an application form from the Guggenheim Foundation. I didn't really think an unknown student composer had much of a chance, but I decided to go ahead and apply. Hoping to get a letter of recommendation from Hanson, I asked his secretary—an old harridan—to see if he would write one for me. Without looking up or stopping whatever she was typing, she replied, yes, he would. I said, "Excuse me, but would you mind going in and asking *him*?" She looked up: "Young man, who do you think had them send you that application?"

Six Elizabethan Songs
(1957–58)

∾

Six songs for high voice and piano (scored for baroque ensemble
    in 1963)
19 minutes
Poetry by William Shakespeare, Ben Jonson, and others
Piano version performed 23 April 1958, Eastman School of
    Music, Rochester, New York; Nicholas DiVirgilio, tenor;
    David Burge, pianist
Baroque ensemble version performed 8 March 1963, First Unitari-
    an Society, Minneapolis, Minnesota; Carolyn Bailey,
    soprano; George Houle, oboe; Jane Burris, harpsichord;
    Jane LaBerge, violin; David Ferguson, cello

The two years at Eastman plus the following one abroad were the happiest and most fulfilling years of my life. When I graduated Bernard Rogers said, "Dominick, you're one student I won't worry about. I'm sure you'll make it." I was still an unknown composer, but my confidence had increased greatly, and I now had an exclusive contract with Boosey & Hawkes, the publisher of Strauss, Bartók, Stravinsky, and Britten. To top it off, I had been awarded a Guggenheim Fellowship. Not surprisingly, we opted to go to Florence.

After touring England, France, Holland, Germany, and Switzerland, we moved into a fine apartment in Florence in a little park along the Arno at Lungarno Torrigiani 7, a block east of the Ponte Vecchio. Little did we know that the following four Florentine apartments we'd occupy over the next forty years would all be within a block of the Ponte Vecchio. I settled down to begin work on my first full-length opera. Around Christmas we had a letter from Nicholas DiVirgilio, a friend and fellow student at Eastman who had sung the tenor role in the premiere of *The Boor*. He wanted me to write some songs for his graduation recital. I went to the bookstore on via Tornabuoni, and from the limited number of volumes of English poetry they had, I bought a copy of Francis Palgrave's *The Golden Treasury* and chose a group of six poems of the Elizabethan era to set. Our apartment had a wonderful view, but the heating left much to be desired: the room where we had placed the piano had none at all. That winter I wore mittens at the piano and could see my breath as I tried out the phrases of these songs.

We returned to the States jobless and spent the summer on my father's hobby farm in York. On the last Friday of September I received a call from the University of Minnesota: Eastman had recommended me for an open theory position. Was I interested? We loaded the car that afternoon and, not being sure where Minnesota was, just headed toward the setting sun. We arrived midafternoon the following Monday, late for the first day of classes, as Dr. Paul Oberg, head of the music department, sternly pointed out. We were hot and tired after a fourteen-hundred-mile drive, and he had failed to arrange lodgings for us as he had promised. I wanted to return to York and have nothing more to do with the Midwest. Much later I used to joke that we didn't really unpack our bags that first couple of years in Minnesota, hoping and praying that a position would materialize on the East or West Coast, certain that remaining in Minneapolis would be artistic suicide for a promising young composer. Gradually that fear evaporated.

In time it became clear that the community was very supportive of the arts. There was a fine symphony (conducted by Antal Doráti), a very good chamber orchestra in Saint Paul, an excellent civic orchestra from which I would shortly receive a major commission. Even the contemporary art museum, the Walker Art Center, which sponsored many modern music events, eventually permitted us to create a small opera company under its aegis. Sir Tyrone Guthrie came to town and built his theater, and I had the good fortune of doing scores for his productions. Mary Ann Feldman, longtime program annotator for the Minnesota Orchestra, accurately observed, "Argento arrived in a Minneapolis on the threshhold of a cultural renaissance." By my fourth year at the university I made the decision that Minneapolis would be home for the rest of my life: should positions from other schools ever be offered I would turn them down. (They were, and I did.)

What appealed most strongly to me about the Twin Cities were the sincerity and commitment of the patrons and consumers of the various arts—particularly music, drama, and painting. In *Art and the Unconscious,* J. M. Thorburn writes: "All the genuine deep delight of life is in showing people the mud-pies you have made; and life is at its best when we confidingly recommend our mud-pies to each other's sympathetic consideration." And in truth, showing people the mud-pies I have made has been a delight. But the second part of Thorburn's statement—about life being at its best when recommending our mud-pies to each other's "sympathetic consideration"—has much greater significance for me: it has been my good fortune not only to practice an art that has been in itself of immense satisfaction to me but also to have landed in a state—namely, Minnesota—in which the art I practice is widely viewed as an essential aspect of life, not merely an ornament or an embellishment. After my arrival in Minneapolis, it did not take long to notice that there seemed to be very little of the posturing that I observed or suspected in other metropolitan areas and scant patience with pretension or faddishness. Corporate patronage was amazing: General Mills, Pillsbury, Dayton's, 3M, and others were members of an organization called the 5% Club, contributing that portion of their profits to the community's welfare.

In 1970, during a visit—for me, a pilgrimage—to Salzburg, Carolyn and I had dinner at the Peterskeller and struck up a conversation with an Austrian sculptor. He had just returned from Pennsylvania, where he had completed an important commission from a church (close, coincidentally, to one in which Carolyn's father had once served as minister). He invited us to his studio the following morning, and during our visit we purchased a small model of a flute player (the life-size original adorns Salzburg's Mirabel Gardens). When we gave him the shipping address, he exclaimed, "Ah, Minneapolis! The Athens of America." I thanked him for the compliment and suggested it might be a bit extravagant. "Oh no," he said. "In our magazines and newspapers all the time we read something about your excellent symphony, your Guthrie Theater, your Walker Art Center, your contemporary opera company, even your Children's Theatre Company. It seems one is lucky to be an artist there."

Thinking about it later, I realized he was not exaggerating. I *was* lucky to be in Minneapolis. I had been warned it would be a mistake to bury myself here, that isolation would not only make the world of contemporary music invisible to me but also make me invisible to that world. In hindsight, I am positive that my decision was a wise one: this far removed from the soi-disant cultural centers, I have been able—for better or for worse—to ignore the trends and fashions of the day. As Peter G. Davis wrote in a 1985 review of my music for *New York* magazine: "*Casa Guidi* is the work of a mature, independent composer who could probably never have developed his creative talent so completely or honed a style this open and clean had he not long ago removed himself from the pressures of East Coast musical politics." Writers and critics frequently make this point, and I could not agree more.

The *Elizabethan Songs*—the very first work I composed upon finishing graduate school—has turned out to be my most performed piece. At present there are at least seven recordings (four American, one English, one German, and one Australian), several of them done with the baroque ensemble arrangement (which I prefer) instead of the original piano accompaniment. It shows up frequently on recitals and seems to be a favorite with voice teachers. Once, during a three-day residency at a University of Wisconsin campus, I was asked to coach voice students working on my songs. At least thirty of them brought in the *Elizabethan Songs*. All but a couple of the singers had photocopies of the music: the two or three printed scores in evidence were library copies. Afterward I described my amusement to Stuart Pope, my publisher at Boosey & Hawkes. "I don't see anything funny about that," he huffed. "You should have refused to coach 'em!" I've been informed that the *Songs* are required repertory for voice majors in Canadian music schools, which to me is more significant than winning the Pulitzer Prize.

Colonel Jonathan the Saint
(1958–61)

∾

Comedy of Reconstruction in four acts and an interlude of waltzes
135 minutes
Libretto by John Olon-Scrymgeour
Performed 31 December 1971, Loretta Heights, Denver, Colorado;
    Mallory Walker, tenor; Matilda Nickel, soprano; Norman
    Johnson, conductor, Denver Lyric Opera

This first full-length opera took three years to complete because I had just started teaching at the university. Preparation for five different courses (a weekly total of nineteen class hours) left precious little time for composing. When act I was finished, Boosey arranged for me to audition it for New York City Opera head Julius Rudel and Phyllis Curtin, one of the leading singer-actresses of the period, who we hoped would take the role of Sabrina. Halfway through my playing, Rudel was called away (I didn't see him again until twenty years later, when he conducted *Miss Havisham's Fire,* his final performance as director of City Opera). Phyllis, however, stayed on to the end.

A year later it was announced that City Opera had commissioned Carlisle Floyd, whose new opera about the Civil War would be titled *The Passion of Jonathan Wade.* John Olon-Scrymgeour, my librettist, stormed into the Boosey office, demanding a copy of Floyd's libretto. The story was virtually identical to ours: John cited nineteen items that clearly seemed inspired by his own original libretto. Obviously Phyllis (who adored Floyd and had had a big success in his *Susannah*) or Bob Holton (vice president of Boosey and Floyd's good friend) had passed the idea on, but we never learned whether Floyd knew of the idea's origin. John was prepared to sue, although being with the same publisher made it awkward. I asked to examine Floyd's score and, confident that the work would fail, discouraged the suit.

It was a flop, as I predicted, but there was a problem I hadn't foreseen: Several years later, with my own opera now completed, I had an interview with John Gutman at the Metropolitan Opera to discuss a possible production. No sooner had I begun recounting the plot than he stopped me. "Wait a minute. Isn't that the same story that Carlisle Floyd's recent opera used?" His interest immediately died. That was the reaction everywhere I auditioned it, until ten years later, when the Denver Lyric Opera took a chance on it. The premiere was a disaster, partly because Denver's promotion department—unaware of the Chekhovian use of the term *comedy*—took the opera's description to heart, scheduled it for a New Year's Eve gala, and advertised an "evening of fun with dinner and dancing to follow." Civil War operas are rarely a barrel of laughs, the food was awful, and I don't dance. Only one other production has ever occurred: the opera department of the University of North Dakota performed it—and quite satisfactorily to my great surprise—in 1976 as a Bicentennial tribute.

At the time of this writing, I am gradually transferring onto compact discs performances of my music (primarily the premieres) that were originally recorded on seven-inch reels of tape and, later, on audiocassettes. Some of these tapes are more than fifty years old and readily susceptible to erosion, flaking, and tearing. Because of this undertaking I heard—for the first time in a quarter of a century—the Denver Lyric's production of *Colonel Jonathan,* and although there are a number of moments I still find worthy of being listened to, it is difficult today to understand why its weaknesses were not apparent to me when I was composing it. It was simply too self-indulgent. The drama, which is relatively slight to begin with, moves forward at a snail's pace, and as a result it is much longer than necessary: four acts that feel even longer than they really are because of a good deal of small talk that I mistakenly believed to be of importance for characterization, local color, and atmosphere. Instead of providing a poetic dimension it was, in reality, just boring. John's idea for a successor to *Colonel Jonathan* came from the famous Ivan Goncharev novel *Oblomov* (the Russians call it their *Hamlet*), about a man who never leaves his bed and is bored with—or afraid of—life. (John's title was *Sebastian's Dream.*) When I showed Bernard Rogers the first-act libretto, he commented, "The trick will be telling the story of a boring man without boring the audience." I didn't think there would be any problem and went on to compose the music for act I. Luckily I was prevented (perhaps the more appropriate word would be *spared*) from completing the opera: after stalling for a year or two, John finally confessed that he hadn't the foggiest idea of what to do for a second or third act, and, moreover, he had lost interest. He, too, it seems, was bored.

Christopher Sly
(1962)

∾

Opera in two scenes and an interlude
70 minutes
Libretto by John Gay Manlove, based on William Shakespeare's
   The Taming of the Shrew
Performed 31 May 1963, Scott Hall Theater, University of
   Minnesota, Minneapolis, Minnesota; Vern Sutton, tenor;
   Mike Carrier, baritone; et al. William Johnson, conductor

*C*hristopher Sly is the result of a request
from the Mu Phi Epsilon music
fraternity. It was designed for the highly limited resources available,
both vocal and technical. The librettist was a theater department
graduate student in my History of Opera course; a young Italian
girl, also a major in theater, created the sets. After auditioning we
wound up with only one decent voice student, the other eight or
nine parts going perforce to amateurs. Fortunately, the sole voice
major was Vern Sutton, whose performance as the Lord was spectacular; this was the first of many roles he would create for me.
The orchestra was a ragtag pickup group conducted by my teaching
assistant, Bill Johnson. Despite the shortcomings among the singers and the orchestra, the show—as one can hear from a tape of the
premiere—vastly delighted the audience. Bob Holton, the vice presi-

34

dent of Boosey & Hawkes who had flown in from New York, said his cheeks ached from laughing.

The origins of the piece as an opera workshop item is fairly obvious, and to my knowledge the opera has never had a truly professional production, although I've yearned to hear it done at least once with fine singers and an adequate orchestra. Tapes I've received from Eastman, Oberlin, and other university productions are nice enough, but both Sly and the Lord need mature voices. The best section is the fugue, which occurs in scene 2 when Sly awakens in the Lord's bedchamber and is reprised later with laughter instead of text as the finale. It attempts to emulate the fugue concluding Verdi's *Falstaff.* Another equally obvious influence is the ensemble-threnody in Britten's comedy *Albert Herring. Sly* has the distinction of harboring my first conscious (and rather simplistic) use of a twelve-tone row: in the interlude each of the thirteen orchestral instruments has a solo cadenza (first and second violins have a duo-cadenza) as the stage is being dressed, in view of the audience, for scene 2. The keys of these twelve cadenzas constitute the row that is used throughout the piece.

Sly was my fourth opera in eight years. At the outset of my career opera was a rara avis. Apart from Gian Carlo Menotti, who had achieved success in the medium (no pun intended), Hugo Weisgall was the only American composer truly committed to the form. Today, fifty years later, virtually every American composer is writing or has written an opera; many have written several. I used to joke that Elliot Carter, given the nature of his musical style, would be the lone holdout, but he too has had his fling. And even Pierre Boulez, who has urged the bombing of all opera houses, may someday yield to the form's allure. This flurry of interest is due, in part, to the enormous increase in number and quality of the opera workshop-studio attached to most universities, conservatories, and major opera companies in the past half century. When I attended Peabody, the opera studio was concerned mainly with preparing and presenting scenes from eighteenth- and nineteenth-century classics. *Sicilian Limes* was denied a production.

A decade later, the opera department of my own University of Minnesota was too inadequate to put on *Sly,* so premieres of my first and fourth operas, by necessity, were produced by ad hoc organizations. In recent decades, however, even operas far more ambitious than *Sly* or *Limes* are routinely performed by music schools or studios. *The Aspern Papers,* originally commissioned for a cast of superstars, has been well done by the University of Illinois opera workshop, the San Francisco Opera Studio, and the Guildhall School of Music and Drama in London, among others. *Postcard from Morocco,* which I regard as a kind of virtuoso piece, has been done by dozens of these non-professional groups. And *Casanova's Homecoming,* which I've been told is rarely performed by the major houses because of its huge cast, has been highly successful in opera studio productions by the University of Cincinnati College-Conservatory of Music (done in Italian at Lucca, where it operates a summer program) and the University of Houston's Moores Opera Center. In 2004, the latter organization will present the revised *Miss Havisham's Fire,* which contains the most difficult operatic role I've ever written. This amazing burgeoning of the opera studio may ultimately become opera's salvation. The enormous expense of running a major opera company may soon bring on that venue's demise, whereas the vocal talent displayed in studio productions—often a match for many of the "stars" one hears in the professional realm and with acting skills at least equal, and frequently superior, to them—can provide a perfectly acceptable operatic experience at a mere fraction of the cost.

An embarrassing footnote: although I was the teacher of a year-long graduate-level course on the history of opera, I was ignorant of the fact that the induction scene of Shakespeare's *The Taming of the Shrew*—wherein the saga of Christopher Sly is begun but left unfinished—had already been treated operatically and had even achieved some success in Germany and Italy. After our premiere, a university colleague, Heinrich Fleischer, told me that in Germany during the 1930s he had attended a *Sly* composed by Ermanno Wolf-Ferrari. I looked it up and found it to be a masterful but strange work. What had seemed to me a brief, obviously comic subject, Wolf-Ferrari had turned into a full-length, disturbing, and pessimistic opera. By coincidence, his *Sly* was probably being rehearsed for its La Scala premiere on the day I was born.

The Masque of Angels
(1963)

∾

Opera in one act
70 minutes
Libretto by John Olon-Scrymgeour
Performed 9 January 1964, Tyrone Guthrie Theater, Minneapolis,
    Minnesota; John Work, baritone; Vern Sutton, tenor;
    Suzanne Styles, soprano; et al. Tom Nee, conductor,
    Center Opera Company

This work marked the beginning of my reputation in the Twin Cities. Originally commissioned by the Ford Foundation for a church in Des Moines, it was rejected because the pastor there was offended that our little religious masque was a comedy and might provoke laughter in his sanctuary (we had driven there and back in a terrible snowstorm on New Year's Eve just to read the libretto to him). Since we had rather hoped our little opus *would* provoke some laughter, it seemed best to withdraw from the commission and allow his church to remain inviolate.

At about that same time we were urging the Walker Art Center to allow us to put on a performance of Britten's *Albert Herring* in the Guthrie Theater with which it was connected. Given the go-ahead, we formed a small group, calling ourselves the Center Opera Company and, on further consideration, decided we had better start out with a work simpler than the Britten opera: John Blow's *The Masque of Venus and Adonis* from 1683, a particular favorite of mine but not very well known. Needing to double-bill it with something, we felt that another masque would be fine: a secular and religious pairing.

In the summer of 1963, through a newspaper ad, Carolyn and I rented a small lakeside cabin in northern Minnesota for one month, where I hoped to compose most of *The Masque of Angels*. To our delight, the entrance arch to the cabin bore the name "Glimpse O' Heaven." In between our biking, boating, and basking in the sun those four weeks, much of the opera got written there. A single performance was scheduled in the Guthrie for the second Thursday in January. With Carolyn playing the lead, the audience loved *Venus,* and, with *Angels* following, the evening was a resounding triumph. Rave reviews the next day in all the local papers, plus a laudatory editorial in the *Minneapolis Star,* created a demand for a repeat performance, which was hastily arranged for Saturday evening and sold out. In the glow of that success, *Albert Herring* was put on a few months later, and Center Opera was immediately established as an important adjunct to the Walker Art Center. For years it was the leading innovative music theater in the country.

I had hoped, with Center Opera securing a place in the cultural landscape of Minneapolis, that it might become for me what Aldeburgh had been for Britten or as the Hilltop Opera had been, briefly, for Hugo Weisgall: a place where one's own works—along with other works one admired and respected—could be properly presented to a discerning and appreciative public. Instead, the company handed me the first of several major disappointments I would experience from it over the years.

A member of Center Opera's founding group was my librettist, John Olon-Scrymgeour, who was also a gifted director. He had staged the debut double bill and a few months later did a coruscating *Albert Herring.* He was as much responsible for our success as anyone. It

was assumed that John would stay on permanently as principal director, and we planned a second season with that in mind. But during
that second season I again had a Guggenheim Fellowship and spent
the year in Florence. In my absence the director of the Walker created
a position of manager for our opera company, and that manager had
a friend who also was a stage director. By the time I returned home
John had been pushed out, the new man installed, and a philosophy
adopted that more often than not allowed the visual qualities of the
productions to overwhelm the musical ones. Well-known modern
painters and sculptors—Robert Rauschenberg, Robert Indiana, and
Jim Dine, among others—were commissioned to design costumes and
sets, seemingly with little consideration of their operatic interests,
sympathies, or experience. The Walker, with its strong emphasis on
contemporary art, evidently regarded the participation of these artists
as only fitting if it were going to subsidize an opera company.

During the third season I distanced myself from the organization and remained totally uninvolved thereafter. The prospect of having an artistic base where I could learn and practice quickly vanished.
Five years later they commissioned, premiered, and toured a kind of
reconciliation work (*Postcard from Morocco*), but despite the extension
of that olive branch and other commissions in later years, the sense of
belonging and camaraderie I had enjoyed that first triumphant season
never returned. But far sadder was another change of philosophy later
on: after a decade of support from the Walker, the opera branched
out on its own. It acquired a board of directors with quite a different agenda and rapidly became just another regional opera company
purveying so-so *Lucias*, *Semiramides*, *Romeo et Juliettes*, often with singers somewhere below the first rank. Lacking outstanding vocalism,
the outdated libretti and ethos of such operas can make for some
unenchanted evenings. What had once been an exciting enterprise
transformed itself into a respectable model of mundanity.

Royal Invitation,
or Homage to the Queen of Tonga
(1964)

∞

Ballet, 40 minutes
Suite for chamber orchestra, 23 minutes
Scenario by John Olon-Scrymgeour
Performed 20 March 1964, Central High School, Saint Paul,
    Minnesota; Leopold Sipe, conductor, Saint Paul Chamber
    Orchestra

B ecause the Des Moines church piece
had fallen through, *The Masque of Angels*
did not turn out to be my first important commission. That distinction came from the Saint Paul Chamber Orchestra. Inspiration for
the ballet came from the First Chamber Dance Quartet, a New York–
based group who performed beautifully through the serious parts
of the opera and uproariously in the "Ballet of the Tie That Binds,"
which brought down the house. Originally intended for dancing,
Royal Invitation was presented by the Saint Paul Chamber Orchestra
almost as a piece of program music: the scenario John had concocted
from a newspaper account of Queen Elizabeth II's coronation could
be followed quite closely in the music. The premiere enjoyed a fine
response. The quartet never got around, however, to doing the work
as a ballet. It has been danced a few times by others (although I have

never seen it), and orchestras frequently perform it. It has been recorded by both a full symphony orchestra and a chamber orchestra.

Tapes of *Masque* and of this ballet were instrumental in getting me another Guggenheim Fellowship, which coincided with a sabbatical I had been granted for 1964–65. Again we spent the year in Florence. I had two projects in hand: a second full-length opera, *Sebastian's Dream* (a rather bold undertaking considering that not the slightest interest had been aroused by my first full-length work, *Colonel Jonathan the Saint,* which had occupied me most of the previous fellowship), and a commission from the Civic Orchestra of Minneapolis for a major symphonic work. During the first few months in Florence I completed the first act of the opera—that was all of the libretto that was finished when we left the United States. No further pages of the libretto ever arrived despite repeated entreaties to John that failed to produce even a letter in return. After the unpleasant machinations at the Center Opera, he had decided to work his way around the world on a Greek freighter. I didn't see or speak with him again until the next season, when he was directing *Masque of Angels* at San Francisco's Grace Cathedral. He gave various excuses for not completing the libretto but promised to finish it soon after hearing the music of the completed first act that I played for him. We never spoke of it again. The opera's being left unfinished was a blessing, I now see, for it probably had as little chance of turning out well as two of John's other full-length libretti—*Colonel Jonathan* and *Miss Havisham's Fire.*

Only halfway through my career did I try my own hand at libretto writing. My first attempt, *A Water Bird Talk,* was highly praised and encouraged me to do *The Aspern Papers* myself when disagreements arose with a different collaborator. When the Minnesota Opera commissioned a new work (*Casanova's Homecoming*), two stipulations were made: that it be a comedy and that I write my own libretto. At the end of the premiere of *Casanova,* Beverly Sills (whose previous involvement with my work had been *Miss Havisham's Fire*) came up to me and said, "Don't you ever let anyone else write libretti for you.

Do them yourself!" I had been so intimidated by John's superior knowledge of theater and dramatic literature that I'd invariably (and mistakenly) deferred to him for the choice of subject and treatment. Of the six subjects he selected, none of the full-length pieces worked out: *Colonel Jonathan* and *Miss Havisham's Fire* were outright failures whereas *Fantasio* and *Sebastian's Dream* were left unfinished and abandoned. Only the seventy-minute *Masque of Angels* and the thirty-minute *Miss Havisham's Wedding Night* are theatrically sound. And I would not deny that I find both of these brief libretti nothing less than minor masterpieces.

Variations for Orchestra
(The Mask of Night)
(1965)

∞

Nocturne, barcarole, burlesca, serenade, toccata, recitative, and
    aria for soprano and orchestra
28 minutes
Lines from various Shakespeare plays about night
Performed 29 January 1966, Coffman Union, University of
    Minnesota, Minneapolis, Minnesota; Carolyn Bailey, so-
    prano; Tom Nee, conductor, Minneapolis Civic Orchestra

The only wholly symphonic work I had
written so far had been *Introduction and
Allegro,* a bit of juvenilia dating from my undergraduate days fifteen
years earlier. The idea for this new work was borrowed from Mahler's
Fourth Symphony, a piece three-fourths orchestral with a solo soprano added for the final quarter. The Mahler had been analyzed in great
detail by Bernard Rogers in the orchestration class I had at Eastman,
and Carolyn had just performed the piece with the Minneapolis Civic
Orchestra the previous season.

    The principal inspiration, however, was Florence. Our newest
apartment, Piazza Pitti 24, was on the seventh floor (no elevator) and
overlooked the broad piazza, the Pitti Palace, and the adjacent Boboli
Gardens. Behind the gardens but not visible from our windows was
a military barracks. Each evening at ten we heard a bugle sound the

Italian equivalent of taps, creating an aural illusion that the solemn music was floating out of the deserted and scented garden. My first reaction to this stimulus was to consider writing an orchestral nocturne, but I didn't think I could sustain a single mood or atmosphere for thirty minutes, the requested length of the work. Perhaps a set of nocturnes displaying a variety of moods? But *what* different moods? Thinking about night brought to mind Juliet's speech, "Come, civil night," and that in turn reminded me of the descriptions of night found in Shakespeare. I decided to select five sentences or phrases about night from various plays to serve as mottoes for different and contrasting sections of music and to end with a setting for voice of Juliet's entire speech. All the sections would be variations on a single theme, just as the poetic quotations varied one theme.

Caught up in all this consideration of night was an operatic role Carolyn once performed: the Queen of the Night in Mozart's *The Magic Flute,* my favorite opera. The first six notes sung by the queen upon her entrance are B-flat, D, F, A, C, E-flat, and to them I added the missing six notes—G-sharp, E, B, G, F-sharp, C-sharp—needed to form a twelve-note row: all very triadic and not unlike taps itself. This phrase became the theme, assigned to solo trumpet and stated three times, each repetition more distant than the previous one. Again Carolyn gave a superb performance, despite the fact that on the January night of the premiere the temperature in Minneapolis fell to twenty-eight degrees below zero.

Variations for Orchestra, in some ways the most attractive, is yet the least performed of my orchestral pieces much to my surprise. It may be that the inclusion of an important part for soprano solo works against it, or, more than likely, it has to do with the fact that Boosey's choice not to publish a study score of this composition, unlike all my later orchestral music, renders it invisible to the eyes of possible performers. Nevertheless, this composition marks a significant development in my music: it is the first piece to be entirely derived from a twelve-note row. It has been pointed out that my use of the serial technique is an anomaly, that the raison d'être of serialism is to ensure the absence of tonality (at least in Schoenberg's concept), whereas the music I compose is rarely atonal.

Then why would I find the technique helpful? In the strict adherence to a series of all twelve different notes—and its attendant mirror image (inversion), and the reverse readings of both (retrograde)—I find I enjoy much greater creative freedom. Some would argue that such an explanation is oxymoronic, since it is absurd to speak of freedom when inflexibility is at the heart of twelve-tone methodology, and departure from the given ordering of notes is proscribed. True enough and I accept that rigor, but what I have found is that by not concerning myself with what note comes next (that, after all, is precisely what the series takes care of), my imagination is completely unhampered and I am free to give my full attention to more important matters, such as shape, texture, and mood.

Put another way: choosing note after note leaves me earthbound; the row permits flight. One of the few positive maxims I have given to students is, "Notes don't matter: it's what they're doing, not what they are." I hasten to add that this approach does not mean that melody is disregarded or even slighted; on the contrary, melody and lyricism are the sine qua non of all of my music. A good composer ought to be able to make a perfectly acceptable melody of any arbitrary collection of notes, be they arrived at through transposing his area code and phone number or the digits on his Social Security card.

A day or two after the premiere of *Variations for Orchestra,* a letter to the editor appeared in the *Minneapolis Tribune.* It had been written by one Bruce Carlson, a law student at the university, someone completely unknown to me at the time. The letter was an encomium for my composition and for Carolyn's singing. And it compared—for the first time—my music to the music of Britten, a comparison that has been inescapable ever since. A decade later I finally met the author of that letter. The former law student was now manager of the prestigious Schubert Club in Saint Paul and as strong a champion of my music as there has ever been. Bruce not only commissioned several major works from me; he also recruited superb performers—Dame Janet Baker, Håkan Hagegård, and Frederica von Stade—to premiere them and helped find funding for recordings. He has also been equally generous and forthcoming with young composers I have recommended to him. In addition to that, he has been a valued confidant and friend.

The Revelation of
Saint John the Divine
(1966)

∞

Rhapsody for tenor, male chorus, brass, and percussion
35 minutes
Book of Revelation
Performed 16 May 1966, Central Lutheran Church, Minneapolis,
Minnesota; Vern Sutton, tenor; Larry Fleming, conductor,
Luther Seminary Choir

The success of the preceding three compositions prompted requests for several new works, among them a commission from Luther Seminary of Saint Paul for a large-scale composition for its choir. The only religious piece I had composed was the oratorio on a text from W. H. Auden's *For the Time Being,* later withdrawn. In all honesty, I must confess that I was attracted more to the dramatic possibilities of the text in the Book of Revelation than to its theology. I was also influenced by the fact that the choir consisted of approximately thirty men: just enough for Saint John's "four and twenty elders" with a male quartet and one or two absentees left over.

I selected passages and arranged them in the form of a rhapsody—certainly John must have been in a state of *raptus* when he wrote—designed for solo tenor (specifically Vern Sutton, whose talent I had come to admire very much in performances of *Christopher Sly, The Masque of Angels,* and, in particular, Britten's *Albert Herring*) accompanied only by brass and percussion. The choice of brass had been suggested by John's reference to the "seven trumpets," although I chose to interpret "trumpets" generically and opted instead for three trumpets, two horns, and two trombones. Two percussion players, piano and harp complete the entire orchestra: the solemnity and gravity of the text discouraged the use of any strings or woodwinds. It ought to be added that what I had in mind—but had not sufficient talent to re-create—was the brilliant description given in Thomas Mann's great novel *Doctor Faustus,* of the fantastic musical work also based on the Book of Revelation created by his fictional composer, Adrian Leverkühn.

An excellent performance of this work was given by the Harvard Glee Club with Jameson Marvin conducting in the school's revered Sanders Theatre. I was very impressed by the serious involvement of the students, which was patent during rehearsals and in deep discussions we had about the piece. My most gratifying memory, however, is the scene I beheld when I visited the green room just before the concert to wish them luck: sixty tuxedoed singers, most of whom were holding, not the music, but an opened Bible, quietly studying its final book.

Around this time there also arose the opportunity to collaborate with Sir Tyrone Guthrie, writing incidental music for a number of his productions. Needless to say, it was invaluable for a budding opera composer to discuss these plays with one of the great stage directors of the time and, even more so, to sit beside him at rehearsal (as he insisted), watching him shape dramas such as Jonson's *Volpone* and, most significant of all, his final production: Aeschylus's trilogy, *The House of Atreus.* Since none of these scores will have individual entries in this catalogue, a word or two about our relationship may be in order here.

Guthrie had directed opera as well as spoken drama, most notably at Sadler's Wells in London and at the Metropolitan Opera. (In a letter he sent me while he was in New York directing *Peter Grimes,* he described the Met as "Bedlam, with very expensive and talented inmates.") He also directed the premiere of Britten's version of *The Beggars' Opera*. We had numerous discussions about opera, and one evening he invited Carolyn and me to his home for dinner, a meal consisting primarily of orange juice and gin. This was lucky since the remainder of the victuals prepared by Lady Judith was virtually inedible—cold pasta smothered in pickles, raisins, and unrecognizable leftovers from the refrigerator. The purpose of our invitation soon became clear: Sir Tyrone wished to read a libretto he had written and offer it for my use. It was the story of a Nativity pageant put on by a theatrical troupe. Rather Pirandellian. His reading made it seem very exciting and Lady Judith herself was moved to tears several times, but when I reread it on my own by the next day's clear light, the *longueurs* outweighed *trouvailles*: one lengthy chorus, for example, consisted of nothing more than that interminable genealogical table wherein so-and-so begat so-and-so.

One afternoon a few days later, I braced myself for the grim task of telling the great man that I didn't think I could use his script. He had me sit at a picnic table behind the theater, read me the entire libretto again, and succeeded once more in making it all seem exciting. Naturally I said I'd reconsider. But in the end it proved to be hopeless: it had been the *way* he read, not *what* he read, that created all the excitement. From hints he dropped, I suspected that he originally offered it to Britten and Britten turned it down.

After Guthrie's death, his biographer, John Forsythe, interviewed us and I mentioned the libretto in passing. He was interested and asked me to tell him about it. I decribed the climactic tableau, in which the chorus encircles two tall ladders forming an inverted V at the apex of which is seated a Murilloesque madonna and child; the child slips from the mother's fingers, falls to the ground, and, being made of plaster, shatters into hundreds of pieces. Forsythe gasped. He said it confirmed a detail that had surfaced in his research: that the shadow hovering over the Guthrie marriage was their childlessness.

The Shoemakers' Holiday
(1967)

∾

Ballad opera
150 minutes
Based on the play by Thomas Dekker; adaptation and additional
     lyrics by John Olon-Scrymgeour
Performed 1 June 1967, Tyrone Guthrie Theater, Minneapolis,
     Minnesota; Douglas Campbell, Len Cariou, Michael
     Moriarity, et al., Minnesota Theater Company

Douglas Campbell, the associate director of the Guthrie Theater, had the
idea of doing Dekker's play as a ballad opera—the simple, lowborn
characters of that comedy having much in common with John Gay's
The Beggar's Opera—and to present it in repertoire during the regular
season. It was a challenge (and a very enjoyable one) to write music
for the large cast of actors, who were, for the most part, unable to
read music. A few of the solo songs (particularly those for Douglas
himself) approach aria status, and the work abounds in ensembles for
which I wanted to compose music with somewhat elaborate harmony
or counterpoint. At first, the music I wrote appeared difficult to the
cast, but in the end it proved completely feasible.

When Guthrie and Campbell first interviewed me in my campus office, they asked to hear something theatrical. I was finishing

Christopher Sly and offered to play some of it for them on the piano. As I did, they stood behind me and, looking over my shoulders, began to sing along, making only a few mistakes. Although the music was not particularly difficult, having been written for students, it wasn't simple hymnal material either; I expressed my surprise at their musical ability. They explained that the sol-fa system had been taught in their English grade schools, and through that study they had acquired some sight-reading skill. Douglas, a superb actor and director, also had a rich baritone voice. I suggested that he would make a fine operatic Figaro. I even made him a gift of a recording of the Mozart opera, hoping to encourage him to consider it. To everyone's surprise, our ballad-opera was the Guthrie's hit of the 1967 season, given over thirty performances to mostly sold-out houses, but since it seems too ambitious or difficult for the average theater company and not sophisticated enough for most opera companies, the piece is rarely performed. Thirty years after the premiere, I was asked by the Plymouth Music Series which of my works I'd like to see presented as a seventieth birthday tribute. I chose *Shoemaker.* It was revived with Douglas again playing Simon Eyre, but this time—to my immense gratification—with a cast, chorus, and orchestra of professional musicians.

Writing incidental scores was a highly educational and beneficial experience, but ultimately it became an unsatisfactory use of my time, since the life of that kind of music extends only through the run of that production. There was one notable exception, however. Douglas was in charge of directing Eugene O'Neill's *S. S. Glencairn,* a quartet of short plays about ships and sailors. He wanted elaborate interludes between the four plays while the scenes were changed in the audience's presence. We agreed that the a cappella group singing of sea shanties and work songs would best serve. Those choral interludes worked so well that I saved them, hoping for a future opportunity where they might enjoy a kinder longevity. That opportunity turned out to be *Jonah and the Whale,* a commission later on from the Plymouth Music Series for a large-scale choral work.

A funny episode occurred in connection with *The House of Atreus*. Guthrie wanted more than seventy-five minutes of choral music, and to provide the appropriate atmosphere, I decided to accompany these choruses with some forty different kinds of percussion. We prerecorded this accompaniment on tape since there was no room backstage for so many instruments and players, and by overdubbing we could use many instruments simultaneously employing only a handful of players. When the production went on tour and played on Broadway, union rules declared that, with more than nineteen minutes of music, *Atreus* was technically a musical comedy. Therefore, if we wished to use prerecorded tape, the musicians' union demanded that a standby orchestra of twenty-nine of their members be hired. Every night of the play's run twenty-nine musicians arrived and played poker or pinochle in the theater's basement while overhead Clytemnestra murdered Agamemnon in his bath and Orestes and Electra plotted to even the score.

Letters from Composers
(1968)

∽

Seven songs for high voice and guitar
28 minutes
Letters of Frédéric Chopin, Giacomo Puccini, and others
Performed 23 October 1968, Macalester College Concert Hall,
    Saint Paul, Minnesota; Vern Sutton, tenor; Jeffrey Van,
    guitar

Vern Sutton and Jeffrey Van (a superb guitarist and composer) asked me to compose a cycle for tenor and guitar, and the form of their commission was a promise to subsidize a commercial recording that was later released on the CRI label. The new cycle was the first vocal work wherein I chose to set prose rather than poetry, a procedure that was to become standard practice for many pieces. Since I felt that the pairing of solo voice and guitar was such an intimate combination, I wanted an equally intimate text to set.

Finding that most poetry seems to be created for public discourse, I began to consider more private forms of writing: letters, journals, diaries, and so on. I have always enjoyed reading the letters of artists, even where the subject was personal and not about their art: reading an artist's own account of his health, anxieties, joys, and

sorrows often sheds significant light on his art. In this case I deliberately chose letters from composers I am particularly fond of, ranging
from Bach to Debussy, and only letters not dealing with music but re-
vealing something about them as human beings. It was not my intention to re-create the composer's musical style so much as to suggest it
in my own musical language.

Thus with Chopin just a hint of nocturne, with Mozart a few
bars of simple Alberti bass, with Schubert a short quotation from one
of his songs. Only with Bach is there anything approaching outright
parody. Looking back over all my pieces now, I see that my attraction
to parody (and sometimes to the outright imitation of earlier periods
or styles of music) has been strong: the spirituals in *Colonel Jonathan*,
the tangos in *The Dream of Valentino*, the bel canto style in *The Aspern Papers*,
the Victorian parlor music in *The Voyage of Edgar Allan Poe*, and so on. No
doubt a more profound explanation could be discovered for this predilection than the one that satisfies me: I do it because I feel a genuine affection for the different kinds of music I parody or imitate, and
I enjoy mixing them in with my own music. It seems to link the little
things I'm doing with the larger world of which I wish to be part.

Six Elizabethan Songs is not in the true sense of the term a song cycle
but is instead a group of songs, having in common only the fact that
the lyrics were drawn from the same period of literature. *Letters from
Composers* (like the earlier *Songs about Spring*) is a real cycle because a
particular theme—the human side of the artist—unites its seven songs.
After *Letters*, all my solo vocal music would continue to use real cyclic
form and be concerned with people. Multiple songs told a story,
like *The Andrée Expedition*, or examined various aspects of a particular
individual, like *From the Diary of Virginia Woolf* and *Miss Manners on Music*,
or explored relationships, like *Casa Guidi* and *A Few Words about Chekhov*.
There is clearly a kinship among these songs cycles, and in some ways
they can be regarded as little operas. An oddity of my output of vocal
music: I have never written a single song, a song intended to stand
alone. Even the very first songs I ever composed, written during my

sophomore and junior years at Peabody, came in small groups—a pair of Emily Dickinson songs and three settings of poems by Walt Whitman.

We invited Tyrone Guthrie to be our guest when *Letters from Composers* was premiered in Saint Paul. He seemed to enjoy it very much and offered a suggestion. He felt that it might be attractively staged with the singer in costume, seated at a desk with candlelight or lamp, quill or pen as appropriate. A few years later I saw it done that way, but I didn't like it. I also witnessed an ill-conceived performance in New York when the singer attempted to play the very difficult guitar accompaniment himself: he kept getting lost—a disaster. *Letters* is often done (and has been recorded several times) by sopranos. I don't care much for that either.

A Nation of Cowslips
(1968)

∞

Seven bagatelles for unaccompanied chorus
18 minutes
Doggerel verse by John Keats
Performed 13 April 1969, University of Minnesota, Minneapolis,
    Minnesota; Charles Schwartz, conductor, University of
    Minnesota Chamber Singers

We purchased our first home, 1919 Mount Curve Avenue, just before I turned forty. When it came on the market I was very taken with it, especially at the bargain asking price, which surprised me. It had been owned by a Dr. Berbos, who had made a lot of money in South Dakota as the doctor who delivered the celebrated Fischer quintuplets. With his windfall, he gave up obstetrics, came to the University of Minnesota to take up ophthalmology, and, receiving his new degree, couldn't wait to get out of Minnesota and set up practice in sunny California (all we found in the house when we moved in were several pairs of skis and four snow shovels).

Carolyn had been distracted during the weeks we were house-hunting: she was getting ready to perform the role of Pamina in the Minnesota Opera's production of *The Magic Flute*. The company had employed Eleanor Steber, a renowned singer Carolyn much admired, to come here to coach the singers. Consequently, the decision to make an offer on the house was left to me. I placed a low bid, which was relayed to the doctor in California; liking the idea that I wrote music for Guthrie productions, he accepted.

The house was a genuine delight to me after thirteen years of living in furnished and unfurnished apartments without a piano. My music studio on the second floor overlooked a large park and proved to be the perfect place to work. There was also a handsome Italianesque garden, all green, terraced, with a pair of stone benches, so in those first few days of occupancy, while Carolyn used the studio to practice Pamina's music, I sat in the garden and out of sheer exuberance composed in a single week of sunshine and contentment *A Nation of Cowslips* at the rate of one bagatelle a day. The poems, written in 1818, are doggerel verses that Keats had included in letters to his friends during a walking tour of England and Scotland. The gay, carefree mood of his letters and poems matched my own so perfectly that it made the composition of these a cappella pieces effortless.

The model for these seven short pieces was Hindemith's charming *Six Chansons,* a work that was highly popular with choruses and madrigal groups everywhere during my student days. By the time I was composing my set, however, Hindemith's work was being heard less often (and I don't believe I've heard it at all in the past three decades), so I hoped *Cowslips* might offer the same singing organizations a comparable substitute or replacement. Unfortunately, I miscalculated its level of difficulty because when I submitted it to Stuart Pope at Boosey, he jokingly (but pointedly) suggested a different title, *A Nation of Sutherlands,* alluding to the need for a chorus of singers as virtuosic as the renowned coloratura Joan Sutherland in order to perform the piece well.

Stuart's complaint was just: I have been told repeatedly by conductors that all my choral music is challenging or outright difficult. Yet I've been told just as often by the choristers themselves that they enjoy singing it. I like to think my choral parts are generally considerate of the singers: the individual lines themselves are never awkward; care is taken to provide reference points for finding entrance pitches; very few demands are made regarding stamina or range. The trouble, I suspect, comes mostly from the free use of tonality or the occasional—very brief—absence of it. This is rarely a problem for instrumentalists, who know just where the right spot is on their fingerboards or which keypad or valve to press in order to produce a particular pitch, whereas singers have to rely on a capricious and far less exact apparatus—vocal cords. To be the equal of an instrumental ensemble in performing difficult contemporary music, a chorus would need to consist of nothing but singers possessing perfect (or at least, relative) pitch, and that is an ideal I have yet to encounter.

Bravo Mozart!
(1969)

∞

Imaginary biography for solo oboe, solo violin, solo horn, and
    orchestra
30 minutes
Short piano works of Wolfgang Amadeus Mozart
Performed 3 July 1969, Northrop Auditorium, University of
    Minnesota, Minneapolis, Minnesota; George Trautwein,
    conductor, Minnesota Orchestra

This work was commissioned for a special summer music course at the university in collaboration with the Minnesota Orchestra. As part of the commission I was expected to give a thirty-minute lecture about its composition prior to the performance, which I did. In one sense *Bravo Mozart!* may be my least characteristic work because it incorporates a few avant-garde techniques (avant-garde of the sixties, that is), such as improvisatory and aleatoric. Both the lecture and the music were love letters to Mozart, whose music, more than any other, has always been the most meaningful and miraculous to me. He is the one composer I feel comfortable proclaiming a genius because his is the only music I truly find unfathomable. I can conceive and I can understand how Bach or Beethoven wrote what they did, and quite frankly I would readily admit that both wrote some boring and uninspired pieces. The only boring thing about Mozart's music is the perfection it never fails to achieve. To me it seems to be the most effortless art ever produced, eternally beautiful, eternally fresh.

Bravo Mozart! is both an imaginary biography of Mozart's brief life and a triple concerto for his three favorite instruments: violin, horn, and oboe. The work is based on several lesser-known piano pieces by Mozart, ranging from the earliest minuet he wrote at age four or five (some commentators have argued that this little G major minuet may really be the work of his father, but I don't believe Leopold was capable of writing anything so perfect) on up to works written shortly before his death. I had not known at the time that Tchaikovsky used a few of the same pieces for one of his own orchestral compositions.

The premiere was well received by audience and soloists—the concertmaster plus the oboe and horn first chairs of the Minnesota Orchestra—and the study score is published, but to the best of my knowledge it has never been performed again, which is disappointing to me only because there are a number of moments in the work that I'm sure would communicate well with an audience. Despite the unqualified success with the performers and listeners at the premiere, I made the mistake of taking seriously some criticism from another composer on the faculty and from my own teaching assistant: both felt that the first, third, and fifth movements were too long and would benefit greatly from some blue-penciling. I tended to accept the criticism because, taking this first opportunity to compose for a fine symphony orchestra, I had been overzealous, writing a thirty-minute work—far longer than had been expected.

I began a revision, crossing out a measure here, a measure there, cutting up and pasting the score and parts (and even the tape of the performance) accordingly. The next day I changed my mind and restored some of the cuts but created new ones as well. Again changing my mind a few days later, I went back, replaced some things, removed others. I became utterly disoriented, unable to make a decision and stick with it. Finally I gave up and slapped together a version as close to the original as I was able to recall. It is probably a blessing that there were no further performances since I doubt whether there is much correspondence any longer between score and parts. Still, it was a valuable lesson: revise at your own peril. As I tried to explain in the preface, the composer who revises his work is no longer the same composer who created it. Except for *Miss Havisham's Fire* (a totally different matter), I was never again tempted to revise a piece.

When Hugo Weisgall's opera *Jenny* was premiered at Juilliard, numerous cuts were suggested by his friends throughout the run. He dutifully incorporated them between performances. They did not improve the work. As Hugo later complained, "Cuts just made it feel longer." A paradox but very true: the logic that bound together the original becomes capriciousness when vital parts are omitted, and the resultant inconsequence makes time seem to pass even less swiftly.

Tria Carmina Paschalia
(1970)

∾

Three Easter lyrics for women's voices (SSA), harp, and guitar
15 minutes
Poetry by Peter Abelard, Sedulius Scottus, and the manuscript
of Benedictbeuern
Performed 11 September 1970, Macalester College, Saint Paul,
Minnesota; Dale Warland, conductor, Dale Warland
Singers

*T*ria Carmina Paschalia was commissioned
by the women's music sorority Sigma
Alpha Iota. I think of it as my "white-on-white" piece because the
female voices, harp, and guitar are rather pale colors: a combination
I thought appropriate for the dead language of the text and for the
Easter subject. It is a kind of companion to its immediate predecessor,
Bravo Mozart!, since it also makes use of a few avant-garde techniques
(among them, tone clusters) not often encountered in my choral
music. Both of these works were strongly influenced by the increasing use of experimental techniques in contemporary music of the
time, much of it finding favor with orchestras and ensembles, if not
with audiences. At first I thought them worth trying out, but it just
wasn't coming naturally and I felt as if I were superimposing them

63

on the music. After these two efforts I realized that for better or for worse it was a mistake to try to be "with it."

I'm certain that the half century I have been writing music has seen more fundamental change—of techniques, aesthetics, philosophy, patronage, even politics—in the composition of music than any comparable period in the past. Until the beginning of the twentieth century there had been a relatively gradual evolution of compositional technique but a certain unanimity of style. In the time of Mozart, most other composers were writing music very much the same as his—just not as good. Wagner was not alone in exploring the world of chromaticism: many other composers were moving in that direction—they were just not as daring.

With the first half of the twentieth century we began to have rival systems that were markedly different and truly antithetical. An admirer of Mozart was not likely to dismiss the work of someone like Salieri because it was a different kind of music but because it was deficient, in workmanship, inspiration, and so on. An admirer of Stravinsky, however, *was* likely to dismiss the work of Schoenberg, not because it was deficient, but precisely because it was a different kind of music. And what had been primarily a schism centered on these two great protagonists in the early half of the 1900s proliferated into more than a dozen factions during the second half, each advocating a kind of music composition seemingly unrelated to anything that had gone before—electronic, aleatoric, improvisational, computer-generated, minimal, and others. There was also much experimentation attempting to graft various elements and aspects of these new approaches to the craft of music composition onto more traditional means because new works that did not exhibit at least some of these features borrowed from the so-called vanguard were brushed aside as reactionary.

Bravo Mozart! and *Tria Carmina Paschalia* represent attempts to make just such an amalgam of a basically conservative approach and a few more-up-to-date appurtenances, and they are, in my opinion, failures. Most of the music I composed up to this point had been a striving (although I didn't think of it that way at the time) to find a style not unlike that which was serving so well for my better-known peers. With the disappointment of these failures came the realization that the important thing was to write as naturally and truthfully as possible, without regard for the trends and fashions currently applauded.

More than a style or unique approach, I wanted to find a voice. A voice—even if it be labeled retrogressive or unfashionable—that was my own. From that point on I was determined to turn my back on the vogues that came and went. No matter how my next work turned out, I was resolved that it would not be indebted in any way to *le dernier cri*—or whatever it was that was rewarding my more successful colleagues with greater attention and eminence. From the vantage point we enjoy today, it would appear that in spite of the teeming experimentation that characterized so much of the music composed in the 1960s and 1970s, very few works were written whose originality could be compared to such imaginative masterpieces from the early decades of the twentieth century as *Pelléas et Mélisande, Le sacre du printemps,* Charles Ives's Second Symphony, *Pierrot Lunaire,* or *Wozzeck.*

Postcard from Morocco
(1971)

∾

Opera in one act
90 minutes
Libretto by John Donahue
Performed 14 October 1971, Cedar Village Theater, Minneapolis,
    Minnesota; Vern Sutton, tenor; Barbara Brandt, soprano;
    Janis Hardy, mezzo; Sarita Roche, coloratura; Yale Marshall,
    lyric tenor; Barry Busse, baritone; Edward Foreman, bass;
    Philip Brunelle, conductor; John Donahue, director

The Masque of Angels made my local reputation; *Postcard from Morocco* made it na-
tional. The *New York Times* sent Raymond Erickson, its principal music
critic, to Minneapolis to cover the premiere, and he gave it a glowing
review. The work was commissioned by the Center Opera Company,
who recorded it on the Desto label a few months after the premiere
and also toured it to Houston, Chicago, San Francisco, and other cities
where it was unfailingly successful with audiences as well as reviewers.
Within a short time it was presented in New York, London, Canada,
and Germany. It has become my most performed opera despite the fact
that many consider it my most "far-out" work for the stage. The seven
years that separate *Masque* and *Postcard* had been a kind of exile, years
during which I did not write the two or three other operas I had hoped
to compose when I envisioned Center Opera as my own Aldeburgh.

Fortunately, the apprenticeship I lost through my quarrel with and withdrawal from the organization was more than balanced by the experience of writing incidental scores for the Guthrie Theater during that same period.

Prior to this commission, I had been considering a work for children with John Donahue for his fine Children's Theatre Company: having seen several of his original productions, I was impressed by his theatrical brilliance. When Center Opera approached me for a new work, I asked him if he'd be interested in writing the libretto for it. He said yes. We had some loose conversations about choosing a subject, then decided it should be an original story, not an adaptation. Eventually he suggested something might be made out of some lines in Robert Louis Stevenson's *A Child's Garden of Verse*: "We built a ship upon the stairs . . . But Tom fell out and hurt his knee, So there was no one left but me." Mystified by the suggestion, I nevertheless agreed and waited for him to produce something.

What he finally gave me was utterly surreal: an untitled piece describing an exotic setting—a group of strangers waiting in a train station—and a dozen or so typewritten pages of dialogue, unassigned to any specific individual. At first I didn't have the faintest idea how to proceed. Ultimately, I rejoiced in the freedom, regarding the text as merely a blueprint, rearranging the lines and assigning them to any character I fancied since I knew exactly who the singers would be, their strengths and weaknesses. (I still have Donahue's original typescript of the libretto showing that I had cut each page into fifteen or twenty horizontal strips and taped the sentences together again in a different order.) Although the piece generally finds favor, I've attended a few performances when paying customers (and a San Francisco reviewer who had previously gushed at great length over *Masque of Angels*) have angrily stormed out.

I spoke before of finding a voice, and I believe *Postcard* is the seminal work in that endeavor. I recognize more of myself in this opera than in any previous composition, as a number of musical traits become clearer: music designed with specific singers in mind (I was familiar with the voices of the seven performers in *Postcard* and tailored the notes to their style of singing and strengths, as I was to do later on for Janet Baker, Frederica von Stade, Håkan Hagegård, Elizabeth Söderström, and Beverly Sills); a penchant for incorporating forms of popular music (blues, cabaret, even bullfight music inter alia); parodies of earlier types of serious music (a lengthy Wagnerian spoof, Viennese operetta, coloratura cadenza with obbligato); manipulation of a twelve-tone technique bearing little resemblance to its inventor's usage; and rampant and unapologetic lyricism. Soon the word *eclectic* began to be applied to me quite consistently in articles and reviews. Not unfairly, I must admit. However, since the word often connotes a disparaging judgment, I would rather be defined less pejoratively— something along the lines of "the whole world of music is his oyster."

I have already pointed out that my favorite opera is *The Magic Flute*. Into it, Mozart emptied a grab bag of just about every musical idiom that he knew: opera buffa, opera seria, coloratura showpieces, a chorale prelude, a march, quasi folk songs, solemn religious choruses, a fugal overture, and even an instrumental musical novelty— the glockenspiel. Without the need to invent anything new, Mozart's genius creates the most eclectic musical work I know, yet how perfectly it serves the libretto's humanity and universality.

I believe artists are prewired either to be innovators or to work within the received tradition. Unquestionably I fall into the latter category and happily so. Without exceeding the boundaries of that tradition I can easily find all the tools I require to write the kind of music I wish to write and to achieve the results I wish that music to achieve. What are the results I wish my music to achieve? I can only repeat Joseph Conrad's words that I emphasized in my preface: *"to reach the secret springs of responsive emotion."* Diaghilev's dictate "Astonish me!" may be fine marching orders for some, but I prefer the far less peremptory commands "Move me" or "Delight me."

A Ring of Time
(1972)

~

Preludes and pageants for orchestra and bells
28 minutes
Performed 5 October 1972, O'Shaughnessy Auditorium, Saint
    Paul, Minnesota; Stanislaw Skrowaczewski, conductor,
    Minnesota Orchestra

A long with a sabbatical leave for the academic year 1971–72, I also had a commission from the Minnesota Orchestra for a work commemorating its seventieth anniversary. The work was completely written in Florence at our third address there, via dei Bardi 58, a spectacular apartment at the foot of the Ponte Vecchio to which we were to return for more than twenty years. Giovanni Bardi, the conte del Vernio, was one of the inventors of opera, and I hoped our address would be talismanic. It was a seventh-floor penthouse (this time there was an elevator) with a fourteenth-century tower (later purchased by Giorgio Armani as a pied-à-terre) attached to the remarkable terrace overlooking the Arno and the entire city. In the distance, the village of Fiesole amid its Tuscan landscape seemed an operatic backdrop. Bell towers of myriad churches dotted the view, and their hourly tolling, reminding one of time's passage, became the idea behind this piece: the ring of time. The orchestra's seventieth anniversary brought to mind the Bible's "three score and ten," the lifespan of a human being: our own ring of time.

Most of the piece was finished when I received a telegram from the conductor saying he'd like me to use all the available players in the orchestra—quadruple woodwinds instead of triple, all auxiliary instruments, and so on. This meant redoing the whole piece, which in itself wasn't so bad, but the problem I hadn't considered at the time was that expanding the orchestra makes the work far more expensive (thus less attractive) to perform.

Skrowaczewski gave the premiere in Minneapolis and, as guest conductor, did the work with the New York Philharmonic. What I remember best about that—my first important performance in New York—was being asked to sit in the front box of the first tier because there was a light above the seat that was used when there was a composer to be recognized. They told me that after my piece ended, the light would be turned on and I was to stand up to be acknowledged. The piece ended. The audience applauded warmly, but since no light came on, I remained seated in the dark. Skrowaczewski, unaware of the custom in Philharmonic Hall, looked around the auditorium in vain, trying to locate me, then gave up, assuming I was not present. At the publisher's party afterward, Stuart Pope said, "A pity that. It would have been a real ovation."

A Ring of Time marks the beginning of a long, fruitful collaboration with the Minnesota Orchestra: half a dozen additional commissions followed it and culminated in my being appointed composer laureate. My relationship with the different conductors varied widely. Between Skrowaczewski (1960–79) and me, there was a touch of courtliness. He has an aristocratic bearing (which carries over into his conducting) and is himself a fine composer of music quite unlike my own. Nevertheless, he gave excellent accounts of two premieres: *A Ring of Time* and *In Praise of Music*. With his successor, Neville Marriner

(1979–86), I enjoyed a much friendlier, more sociable relationship. It was his idea to have me write a work for mezzo and orchestra. His first choice had been Janet Baker, and when it turned out that she was unavailable, he turned to Frederica von Stade. The result was *Casa Guidi,* which he premiered and toured to Carnegie Hall, the Kennedy Center, and various cities. He gave the London premiere with the Royal Philharmonic and ordered a reduced version for his Academy of St. Martin in the Fields orchestra. He wanted me next to do a concerto for cello or violin, but I was busy with an opera at the time.

Relations with the next director, Edo de Waart (1986–95), were glacial. He had been hired to be the hatchet man that Neville was unwilling to be, with a mandate to weed out the weaker musicians in the orchestra, a task he carried out punctiliously, earning the epithet the Dutch Cleanser. As conductor designate, he was invited to the Minnesota Orchestra's concert at Carnegie Hall when Neville and Flicka (as friends and fans call her) presented *Casa Guidi.* Not precisely a diplomat, he bluntly informed the enthusiastic board members at the party following the concert that he disliked my kind of music. Against my wishes (and no doubt his), only one work of mine was performed during his tenure. David Zinman, artistic director of the Minnesota Orchestra's Sommerfest (1993–96) and a former student of mine, was exactly the opposite. He was responsible for *Valentino Dances* and *Valse Triste.* Best of all was Eiji Oue (1995–2002), who had a genuine affinity for my music and recorded two CDs that include excellent performances of eight of my orchestral works.

Jonah and the Whale
(1973)

~

Oratorio for tenor, bass, narrator, mixed chorus, and instru-
    mental ensemble
60 minutes
Patience, or Jonah and the Whale (anonymous medieval English, circa
    1360), Book of Jonah, traditional work songs and sea
    shanties
Performed 9 March 1974, Plymouth Congregational Church,
    Minneapolis, Minnesota; Vern Sutton, tenor; Leroy Lehr,
    bass; Philip Brunelle, conductor, Plymouth Music Series
    Festival Choir

N ot counting the withdrawn *Temptation
of Saint Joseph,* this work, commissioned
in honor of the tenth anniversary of the Plymouth Music Series, is
my fourth large religious piece. In compiling this catalogue it has
surprised me to see just how much religious music I have written.
Even as an undergraduate I had struggled for weeks over a cantata
based on the Book of Job before realizing that the endless chain of
woes that beset him was resulting in a very glum composition, far
beyond the skill of the green composer I then was. (Job's tribulations
could also defeat a masterful composer like Dallapiccola: in Florence
I attended the premiere of his *sacra rappresentazione* on that unfortunate
biblical figure and realized that the problem was not a question of
talent but the unlovable subject.)

When viewing my religious pieces as a whole, it will be obvious that optimistic, even humorous, texts predominate. Much as I prize the requiems by Mozart and Verdi, I failed repeatedly to get anywhere with a Mass for the Dead that I wished to compose to honor my father. The kind of religious music I have written resembles more the *Messiah* type than the *Elijah* type: cheerful and uplifting rather than monitory and penitent. *The Revelation of Saint John the Divine,* which was chosen more for that text's dramatic opportunities than its theology, is the exception. I only recently realized that much of my religious music uses macaronic texts, a mixture of both secular and liturgical language: in *Jonah* we have sea shanties, medieval English poetry, and verses from the King James and Latin Vulgate Bibles; in the *Te Deum,* Saint Augustine's prayer and Middle English poems; in *Spirituals and Swedish Chorales,* the title is self-explanatory.

There was a serious flaw in *Jonah* that I failed to foresee in time. The medieval English poem provides a marvelous, hair-raising description of the storm God sends to provoke Jonah's ejection from the boat. In my enthusiasm to indulge in some fancy tone-painting, I asked the chorus and orchestra to outdo themselves in dissonance and volume, creating a tremendous din. Left out of my consideration was the poor narrator, who, describing the ferocious storm, must shout hundreds of words above the ruckus. Even powerful amplification proves futile. Only lowering the performers' decibel level seems to work and that, of course, spoils the effect.

Jonah stands at the beginning of a long association with Philip Brunelle and the Plymouth Music Series. A good number of pieces were commissioned by the Music Series itself or for the Plymouth Congregational Church choir. It has been a fine example of the benefits a composer might enjoy by establishing himself in a community where his work is wanted rather than rushing off to New York or San Francisco and scrambling for a position among fifteen thousand other composers. I have always urged graduating students to look for a community that can use what they do, where they can be made to feel like useful, contributing members of society.

The importance of this notion did not strike me when I first arrived in the Twin Cities, but over the years it became obvious. In this area alone I have been asked to write music (and several times in most cases) for the Walker Art Center, the Saint Paul Chamber Orchestra, the Schubert Club, the Minnesota Orchestra, the Minnesota Opera, the Guthrie Theater, the Dale Warland Singers, the Plymouth Music Series, the Fargo-Moorhead Symphony, the Civic Orchestra of Minneapolis, and the University of Minnesota, plus many individuals. I was made to feel that they all wished to have music from me. Like a doctor or teacher, I was being paid for services needed and rendered. It was not at all like a grant awarded by a foundation endowed by some long-dead philanthropist who would never hear or care about what one wrote. Of course these foundations serve a noble purpose by letting artists know that their work is estimable or meritorious. Nevertheless, their benefactions are, at heart, a form of charity. To me, it is infinitely better to know that one's work is desired or wanted. That is a form of love.

To Be Sung upon the Water
(1973)

∾

Barcaroles and nocturnes for high voice, clarinet, bass clarinet,
    and piano
25 minutes
Poetry by William Wordsworth
Performed 20 October 1974, University of Minnesota,
    Minneapolis, Minnesota; Clifton Ware, tenor; Joseph
    Longo, clarinets; Paul Freed, piano

After tenor Mallory Walker created the title role in my Civil War opera, *Colonel Jonathan the Saint,* he asked me to compose a song cycle for him. As with *Letters from Composers,* a commercial recording was guaranteed in place of a monetary commission, and the president of the record label Desto, which had recently issued *Postcard from Morocco,* agreed to take it on. Unfortunately, the recording sessions were arranged during one of our extended stays in Florence, and I never learned why Mallory was not asked to record it. Desto had chosen John Stewart, whom I had never heard and, by being abroad, I had no opportunity to coach. The record, as a result, was far from what I would have wished it to be. All very disappointing, I thought, but no use crying over spilled milk and soon I forgot all about it. Only later did I realize that most singers wishing to program the work listened to that recording and modeled their performance on it, assuming, I suppose, that it had had my approval. To this day, because of that recording, adequate performances of the piece are rare. Regrettably, the published score does not make it clear that the work is for tenor voice. Instead, it says "for high voice," which means soprano or tenor. (As the publisher reminded me, "We mustn't forget the ladies!") Consequently, sopranos also perform it, and several have recorded it as well, to my displeasure, duplicating the original recording.

The form of the work resembles nested arches. The two central songs are "In Memory of Schubert" and "The Swan," the latter being an analogical reference to that composer. Flanking these songs is a pair of contrasting songs about music heard on the water, the first tranquil, the other ominous. Flanking this pair is another pair describing the lake at evening and the lake at night. And flanking these are the prologue and epilogue: the former speaks of the confusion that can exist distinguishing shadow from substance, and the latter is one of Wordsworth's best-known sonnets, "The World Is Too Much with Us." The cycle's title is, of course, an allusion to Schubert (one measure of "Auf dem Wasser zu singen" is quoted), and the use of clarinet along with piano for accompaniment was suggested by his "The Shepherd on the Rock."

My illusion of becoming a pianist was dispelled in that first year at Peabody Conservatory, although by immediately refocusing on composition I never regretted it. Even though I would never enjoy that dreamed of career, I played piano well enough for my own pleasure and to accompany recitalists, to coach singers, and to audition my pieces. (Unhappily, my mastery of the last-named skill, which often required me to sing, was rather less than awe-inspiring. After I auditioned *Colonel Jonathan* for the director of Indiana University's opera program, he said, "You realize, I hope, that if Mozart had auditioned *Figaro* like that, no one would ever have produced it.") But I did feel some regret over failing to become accomplished on a different instrument. One of the requirements for a master's degree in composition was the demonstration of a certain ability on an instrument other than piano. Being left-handed ruled out stringed instruments for me. The valves and slides of brass instruments also favored right-handers. That left only woodwinds and I chose the clarinet, thinking it the easiest. I studied the instrument with an excellent teacher, Sidney Forrest, and by the end of one year's instruction I was playing so well that he urged me to become a professional clarinetist. Nothing could have changed my course set on being a composer, and so, upon obtaining my master's, I returned my rented clarinet to the music store.

Later I wished I had purchased the instrument and continued to practice it, for I had become fond of the instrument and missed the enjoyment I might have had of playing, limited as I was, in amateur ensembles and orchestras. It is the only orchestral instrument for which I have written solo works: the extended role it has in this song cycle as well as a full-fledged concerto. One unexpected result of my familiarity with the clarinet has been that the parts I wrote for that instrument in my full scores were always the least demanding among the winds. It was years before I became aware of what I was doing: unconsciously I was mentally fingering the clarinet part as I orchestrated, and anything I found too hard to play I simplified. My ignorance of the other winds allowed their parts to be more adventurous. It is not surprising to me that Hindemith, who could play virtually every instrument, was relatively restrained in his orchestral writing, whereas Stravinsky, who only knew piano, wrote far more challenging instrumental parts.

A Water Bird Talk
(1974)

~

Monodrama in one act
45 minutes
Libretto by the composer, based on Anton Chekhov's *On the
Harmfulness of Tobacco* and John James Audubon's *Birds of America*
Performed 19 May 1977, Brooklyn Academy of Music, Brooklyn,
New York; Vern Sutton, tenor; Ian Strasvogel, conductor,
Orpheus Chamber Ensemble

This piece has an unusual origin. Whenever composition students expressed
the desire to compose an opera, I encouraged them to begin with
a short chamber-size work, preferably a comedy (I thought it easier
for a beginner to handle than serious drama), and, if possible, to
write the libretto themselves since collaboration with an experienced
librettist was generally out of the question. When asked where to
start, I usually suggested an adaptation from one of the short plays by
Chekhov or Cervantes, or something comparable and—very important, as one will see from later remarks—free of copyright restraints.
I often directed students to Chekhov's *On the Harmfulness of Tobacco* as
a sensible choice because of its single character and brevity. But after
a week of struggling with it, the student invariably returned hopelessly baffled by the problem of transforming the play into a libretto.

I decided to make a libretto of it myself as a demonstration and give it to those students who found the adaptation task too daunting. But even though the libretto I gave them was far simpler than the text I later set to music myself, the students still floundered, finding the situation and character too difficult, and most of them moved on to something else. I eventually accepted the fact that the setting of my sample libretto to music was much too challenging for a beginner, and I put it away and stopped suggesting it.

I learned that the National Endowment for the Arts had turned down my application to compose a monodrama on Samuel Beckett's *Krapp's Last Tape*. (I had chosen this play because of the possibility of the protagonist dialoguing with himself: I particularly wanted to hear Vern Sutton singing duets with Vern Sutton.) The reason I was rejected surprised me: the author refused to grant his permission because his son, who fancied himself a composer, expected to use the material for an opera of his own. (I have never learned whether he did.) The NEA said I still might receive a grant if I chose material or subject matter that did not present any copyright issues. In place of the Beckett monodrama—time being so short—I submitted to the NEA the Chekhov libretto that my students had been unable to tackle.

I got the grant, and after the monodrama was composed and performed all my regrets over not having obtained the rights to *Krapp's Last Tape* faded: I think *A Water Bird Talk* has proved to be a far wiser choice. Considering the somewhat makeshift manner in which this piece came into existence, it may be surprising to learn that it is my one stage work that I regard as wholly and utterly satisfying: there is not a word or note in it I would wish to change. I think this is due to the correspondence and compatibility of action, text, and music that I see in it and that in turn may be due to my acting as both composer and librettist for the first time. *The Aspern Papers* and *Casanova's Homecoming,* for which I was the librettist, also display a heightened degree of unity, although the synergy is not as total as in *A Water Bird Talk.* That, perhaps, may be because they are three and four times as long, respectively, as the monodrama.

Writing my own libretto, I discovered, had one unexpected advantage. While actually composing, whenever I felt that a musical section would benefit from being a bit longer than the given text required, I could provide the additional words or phrases without wasting time to consult (or seek the approval of) a collaborator. Contrarily, whenever I saw merit in not going on musically for as long as the text seemed to demand, I could abbreviate or make adjustments on my own. Best of all, whenever I felt that a musical idea or development I hadn't foreseen could add something to a given scene—even though the libretto made no allowance for it—it was relatively easy to find an accommodation. I undertook the role of librettist for *A Water Bird Talk* out of necessity. I had no great illusions about my ability, but I had come to an important conclusion about the writing of operas: usually the music has to adjust itself to the words, but there are times when the words ought to adjust themselves to the music, and to do that the composer needs to control both the words and the music. Wagner understood this so well: the latter half of act 2 of *Tristan und Isolde* consists of half an hour of glorious music and little more than two words (or minor surrogates thereof)—he merely repeats her name and she repeats his. I doubt if even the finest poet-librettist would have thought of that as a possible text for a great duet.

The Wagner example, which is a rare case, reminds me of the most frequent question I have been asked over the years: in an opera, what's written first, the words or the music? Some of the confusion probably comes from the knowledge that many popular songs are composed as melodies to which words are added afterward. Or perhaps misleading are those letters of Verdi or Puccini asking a librettist to please give them four or eight lines of "tum-ti-tum-tum-ti-ti-tum" to fit a new musical idea they have or to extend a particular section: this, naturally, would apply only to very short sections of the opera. To me, it would be the height of absurdity to compose two or three hours of abstract music and then go back and stick words on every note, making up a story as one goes along. The words *must* come first, since the very tone, texture, color, and speed of the music are dependent on the text that it wants to underscore, interpret, or illustrate.

From the Diary of Virginia Woolf
(1974)
∾

Eight songs for medium voice and piano
35 minutes
Excerpts from Virginia Woolf's diaries
Performed 5 January 1975, Orchestra Hall, Minneapolis,
   Minnesota; Janet Baker, mezzo; Martin Isepp, piano

Bruce Carlson, manager of the Schubert Club, booked soprano Jessye Norman for a recital in 1974 and commissioned me to write a cycle for her. By the time I had searched for and found a suitable text to fit her unique talents (excerpts from Sappho), she canceled. I learned she was going to be replaced with Beverly Sills, for whom I felt Sappho was unsuited. Instead, I thought to compose something "actressy," perhaps a gallery of Shakespearean heroines: Ophelia, Cleopatra, and so on. I can't remember why Sills also had to cancel, but to my good fortune she was replaced with British mezzo Janet Baker.

For Janet, both Sappho and "actressy" were plainly wrong. Bob Moore, a friend of ours in the English department at the university and a great fancier of female voices, suggested the interludes describing the gradual rise of the sun over the sea's horizon in Virginia Woolf's

The Waves. Wanting to know more about Woolf's intentions in the use of that image, I looked up *A Writer's Diary*. As soon as I began reading, it struck me that the diary itself was more interesting than Bob's original idea. The hardest part was picking which entries to use; I reduced my favorite but unwieldy dozen down to eight and arranged them chronologically from the earliest to the final entry, spacing the others in between about five years apart.

The finished score was sent off to Boosey, and both Baker and her accompanist, Martin Isepp, received a copy of it months before the date of the premiere. However, both were touring independently in different parts of Europe and North America, and they had had no opportunity to go over the piece together until they arrived in Minneapolis Thursday evening before the Sunday afternoon recital. They worked Friday and Saturday and requested that I not attend any rehearsal until Sunday morning.

When I arrived at the brand-new Orchestra Hall that Sunday morning, I was introduced to Janet and Martin, and they asked if they should go through one song at a time and then discuss it, or sing the cycle straight through. I said I preferred having them do the entire thing first without any interruptions from me. When they finished, I was speechless, utterly flabbergasted. It was perfection. Two days before, they had never done the piece, and now I had just heard a performance that to this day has never been surpassed. Even the premiere that afternoon was not quite as good as that first run-through. Janet asked me to come up and give them my criticism. I went onstage and said, "I have nothing to tell you except that I'm a blubbering mass of gratitude and will never be able to thank you enough." I took my leave and let them go on to rehearse the rest of the program alone. Unbeknownst to them, the engineer, who was setting balances and microphone placements to tape the recital for a later radio broadcast, was surreptitiously recording the rehearsal. Janet is distinctly heard on that tape whispering to Martin as I walked offstage, "What a lovely man!"

That following April, weeks before the Pulitzers were announced, Hugo Weisgall phoned: inside information had it that *Woolf* had won. I didn't believe him. A week later Stuart Pope at Boosey called to say he, too, had heard the rumor. I still didn't believe it. He promised he would phone at 5 (Minneapolis time) the morning the *New York Times* published the winners' names. On the eve of announcement day, I sat by the phone all night, unable to sleep, reading Will Durant's *Story of Philosophy*. At 5, nothing. At 6, nothing. By 8, still nothing. Convinced I hadn't won, I went to bed. Soon after 9 a.m. the phone rang. I no longer remember what had delayed him, but Stuart said yes, it was true: *Woolf* had won.

I feel a little sorry for the composer resident in New York City, Los Angeles, or some comparable megapolis winning a Pulitzer. No doubt a substantial amount of publicity is received. But being awarded the prize in Minneapolis created a virtual blitzkrieg of media attention. By noon, vans from the four local TV stations were parked in front of our house with long black cables snaking across a small patch of lawn, onto the porch, in through the open front door, up a staircase on which half a dozen radio and newspaper reporters, plus stringers for the AP and UPI, were jostling for position, and into my second-floor studio, where unimaginative videographers insisted on filming me seated at the piano, pencil in hand, focusing on a sheet of music manuscript, pretending to be composing. (I have never understood their fondness for this pose. It always reminds me of a safari-suited, pith-helmeted hunter, cradling a rifle in his arms, with one foot resting lightly on an elephant's carcass.) The following morning during a tremendous downpour our doorbell rang and Carolyn answered to find our postman in slicker and plastic-protected cap, rain streaming off his visor, down his glasses, face, chin, holding a tall stack of soggy letters, cards, and mailgrams. Smiling but bemused he handed her the pile and said, "I guess this means he's going to be famous."

The Voyage of Edgar Allan Poe
(1975–76)

∽

Opera in two acts
125 minutes
Libretto by Charles Nolte
Performed 24 April 1976, O'Shaughnessy Auditorium, Saint
     Paul, Minnesota; Philip Brunelle, conductor, Minnesota
     Opera Company

The dean of the College of Liberal Arts at the University of Minnesota, Frank Sorauf, was president of the Minnesota Opera in 1974, and it was his idea that the university commission me to write an opera in honor of America's Bicentennial. Tossing around for a subject of more than simple national or historical interest (however chauvinistic the topic, I wanted the opera to be about something that Europeans were also familiar with), I finally settled on Edgar Allan Poe because he seemed the first American artist to achieve international significance. I began seriously researching his life and works, and it occurred to me that something might be done akin to Puccini's *Il trittico* or Offenbach's *The Tales of Hoffmann*.

While still vacillating over which stories I might use and how to connect them, I saw a performance on campus of *A Night at the Black*

Pig, Charles Nolte's play about August Strindberg. It had exactly the mood and dramaturgy I wanted for the opera. Charles was not only an accomplished and respected actor and playwright but a highly knowledgeable opera enthusiast as well. He became excited when I told him about the mysterious voyage that led to the author's death—as bizarre as any story Poe himself had written—and was eager to do the libretto. Shaping a libretto, given the many characters in Poe's writings and in his life, plus the poetry that we might incorporate, was a lengthy affair, requiring quite a few months before the libretto would be exactly what I wanted. Since I did not want to start composing until we had a complete acceptable text, I decided to work on something else to fill the time. That time filler turned out to be *From the Diary of Virginia Woolf.*

Given a year's leave, I began *Poe* on Columbus Day, 1974—an auspicious day to begin a voyage—continued it in Florence the following summer, and orchestrated it during the winter of 1975–76 ("From a Composer's Journal," a more fully detailed account of the composition of this work—from conception to completion—will be found at the end of the catalogue). Rehearsals went well until the tenor playing Poe—the role had turned out to be long and taxing—grew frustrated and began having memory lapses. Two days before the premiere, his nerves completely frayed, he blew up and walked off the stage, threatening to pull out. I asked Vern Sutton (who was playing the smaller role of the doctor) if he thought he could take over the lead in forty-eight hours. He probably could have done so, but tempers quickly cooled and the premiere came off smoothly and was a great success, garnering rave reviews in *Time* ("Poe is Argento's eighth opera and as fine as any ever written by an American"), *Opera News* ("Looking back in decades to come, the spring of '76 may mark the coming of age in American opera"), *Newsweek* ("A significant step forward in the cause of daring and originality"), the *New Yorker* ("a distinct success"), the *New York Times* ("a rich, mature, and substantial creation"), and many other national newspapers. A year later, it ran for a week at a Baltimore theater less than a mile from Poe's grave.

Although productions in Germany and Sweden continued its success, nothing more was heard of the opera in the United States for the next thirteen years and I was resigned to its disappearance. Then in the late eighties, Ardis Kranik, the artistic director of Lyric Opera of Chicago, dreamed up a project titled "Toward the Twenty-first Century." Her plan was to present a masterpiece of twentieth-century opera each season from 1990 to 2000. It would be a gross understatement to say I was stunned when she said she wanted *Poe* to be the opening work. When I expressed my astonishment, she explained that she had invited many reviewers and opera house directors to submit their suggestions: *The Voyage of Edgar Allan Poe* was the hands-down favorite. I was amazed: here was an opera that had been seen and heard in only two lesser American cities—Saint Paul and Baltimore—then vanished for more than a decade, yet it had amassed this big underground reputation.

For the Chicago revival, Frank Galati directed the most exciting production an opera of mine has ever had. I think Poe himself would have enjoyed the histrionics and bizarreness of it immensely. Christopher Keene, director of New York City Opera, conducted the Chicago revival (and led the same production a year later in Dallas). It seemed incredible to him that the work had never been done in New York (and to this day, it still has not been). To arrange its premiere there and to record the work were among his plans when he died. Since then, *Poe* has once again lapsed into obscurity.

In Praise of Music
(1977)

∞

Seven instrumental songs for orchestra
30 minutes
Performed 23 September 1977, Orchestra Hall, Minneapolis,
    Minnesota; Stanislaw Skrowaczewski, conductor,
    Minnesota Orchestra

A *Ring of Time* was commissioned for the
Minnesota Orchestra's seventieth an-
niversary, and *In Praise of Music* was commissioned for its seventy-fifth.
The original subtitle—*Seven Songs for Orchestra*—was an unfortunate
choice. The Friedheim Awards presented at the Kennedy Center
alternate annually between orchestral music and chamber music.
Submissions for the competition (as are Pulitzer Prize nomina-
tions) are made only by presenters or publishers. The orchestral
competition is limited to purely instrumental music, without solo
voices or chorus, and this was the category in which Boosey correctly
nominated *In Praise of Music.* Seeing the subtitle, the judges assumed
"songs" meant voices and disqualified the piece without bothering
to notice that no singers were involved. Had I known that the work
would be disqualified on those grounds, I would have changed the

subtitle to what it is now or, better yet, simply omitted it. Years later, *Fire Variations,* a composition not nearly as strong in my opinion, did become a finalist in the Friedheim competition, leading me to think that *In Praise of Music* might have done even better had that blunder been avoided.

In 1979 the piece was performed at Carnegie Hall by the Rochester Philharmonic conducted by David Zinman. A day or two earlier, *The Boor* had been presented by one of the small opera companies in New York City, and a day or two later *Miss Havisham's Fire* premiered at the New York City Opera. The *New York Daily News* ran an article reviewing all three events under the charming headline "Dom's Winning Week." The instrumentation of the seven pieces is, *ad seriatim*: tutti, brass alone, tutti, strings alone, tutti, woodwinds alone, violins alone. All of the songs are based on a fragment of music—ranging from a brief phrase to a complete melody—from various cultures and eras. Like most of my orchestral music, it is virtually unknown in the concert hall, although as I write this a recording of it is about to be released by the Minnesota Orchestra.

Since there is no text, why "songs" instead of seven "melodies" or seven "pieces" for orchestra? The reason goes back to my ideas about the origins of music. I do not accept the pretty myth crediting Apollo with the creation of music when he strummed the dried tendons stretched across a tortoise shell, thereby inventing the lyre, or another myth giving that honor to Pan who—by blowing across a handful of broken, hollow reeds—invented the syrinx, because both imply that our earliest music was instrumental. To the contrary, I believe it was vocal, originating in the throat and invented long before there was a verbal language capable of communicating feelings from one soul to another.

My hypothesis is that some prehistoric parent discovered that low, soft, crooning sounds calmed a fretful, ailing child and brought comforting sleep—the first lullaby; if the child worsened and died, wailing and keening gave vent to unbearable pain and sorrow—the first lament; were the child miraculously restored to health, reverent, solemn tones of gratitude and praise had to be rendered to an inscrutable power—the first hymn; and when everything was going well, the mindless humming that happiness provokes unawares—the first glee. These antique usages of music are with us still: the troubled mind yearns to be soothed; the despairing heart needs expression for emotions too deep for words; the uncertain soul must appeal to something beyond itself. Instruments came along later, at first as imitations of the voice; in time they learned to go higher or lower, be louder, produce different colors, sound several tones simultaneously, but they still manifest those ancient customs of music that the human voice discovered long ago and they still delight in doing what it did: singing.

The score is inscribed with these lines from Walter Savage Landor:

> There is delight in singing, though none hear
> Beside the singer; and there is delight
> In praising, though the praiser sit alone.

Miss Havisham's Fire
(1977–79)

∞

Opera in two acts, plus a prologue and epilogue
163 minutes
Libretto by John Olon-Scrymgeour, after *Great Expectations* by
    Charles Dickens
Performed 22 March 1979, State Theater, Lincoln Center,
    New York City, New York; Rita Shane, soprano; Gianna
    Rolandi, soprano; Alan Titus, baritone; Suzanne Marcy,
    mezzo; Julius Rudel, conductor, New York City Opera

O ne afternoon in the summer of
1977 I came in from the terrace
of our Ponte Vecchio apartment to answer the phone. Stuart Pope,
calling from New York, said, "Are you sitting down?" I sat. "I've
been talking with Beverly Sills and Julius Rudel. They'd like you to
compose a piece for her last operatic appearance and his final appearance as director of City Opera. I'll set up a meeting for when
you return from Florence." Sills had a tentative suggestion for a libretto: Empress Carlotta of Mexico. I found a copy of *Imperial Madness*
at a Florentine bookstore and thought the subject was not without
possibilities. Because some bizarre situations in her story reminded
me of our successful previous collaboration, I again asked Charles
Nolte to write the libretto, which he began immediately, titling it *The
Phantom Empress.*

That fall I invited Sills to lunch during a visit she paid to Minneapolis. The libretto was not finished nor was any music yet written, so she asked if I had any alternative ideas to the Carlotta opera. I told her about John Olon-Scrymgeour's libretto *Miss Havisham's Wedding Night* but explained that it was only a short monodrama and hardly the right vehicle for her departure from the stage. Sills responded enthusiastically to the idea of an opera based on the character of Miss Havisham—a *folle d'amour,* she called her, not unlike many of the operatic heroines she had portrayed during her career. She wondered whether a full-length opera could be written about her. I told her I thought it could and she immediately said: "Let's do that instead!"

I must admit that, at first, I was disappointed about dropping the Carlotta idea because two or three scenes had already been shaping up quite interestingly in my mind, but the more I thought about the possibilities with Dickens the more I was drawn to it. Since the Havisham idea had been John's, I had to ask him to write the libretto and, with great awkwardness, tell Charles we were abandoning Carlotta. Charles did finish his libretto with the aid of an NEA grant, and I still think it would make a fine opera.

Unhappily, *Miss Havisham* in its first manifestation did not, despite the great pains I had taken with the music, which I am convinced was the best I had ever written. It was impossible to judge the audience's reaction on opening night because, by prior arrangement, homage to Julius Rudel on his final appearance as director and principal conductor was tacked on to the curtain calls: dozens and dozens of singers who had performed at City Opera over the years had been invited for the occasion, and while the maestro was taking his bow they poured up the aisles, clapping, and joined him and the cast on the stage. All of them, plus orchestra and an audience on its feet, participated in a rousing "Auld Lang Syne" and much cheering.

The excessive length of the opera (two eighty-plus-minute acts as well as a thirty-minute intermission) caused it to run very late, so we were sure there would be no review in the *New York Times* the following morning. Feeling confident, we slept in, had a late breakfast, enjoyed a leisurely stroll through Central Park (it was a gorgeous day), lunched at the Metropolitan Museum of Art, checked out a few exhibits, and then returned to our hotel for a brief nap. Around 4 p.m. the phone rang. Jean Golden, Stuart's secretary at Boosey & Hawkes, was calling and with a bright smile in her voice asked how we were and how it felt to have the *New York Times* put *Miss Havisham* in the same category as Britten's *Billy Budd*. I told her I guessed it would feel great, but surely the review wasn't out yet . . . She suddenly became embarrassed and flustered: thinking we had already seen the papers, she had meant her words to be consolatory.

As it turned out, Jean was breaking the news to us that the *Times* had thoroughly panned the opera, just as it had panned *Billy Budd* at the Met some months before. Other newspapers and journals were mixed and in some cases very positive. For example, the *Wall Street Journal*'s review, headlined "A New Opera to Delight the Imagination and Ear," praised the piece for being "a musically absorbing, seamlessly crafted work . . . How many contemporary operas have done that lately?" Several other critiques were in the same vein, but as everyone knows, in matters of artistic survival, the up-or-down position of the *New York Times*'s thumb is the only opinion that counts. There was no getting away from it: *Miss Havisham's Fire* was the biggest failure of my career, and no other failure before or since has hurt nearly as much.

I sometimes wonder how different my career might have been had we gone ahead with the Carlotta opera instead of *Miss Havisham*. Obviously the many complimentary reviews of *The Voyage of Edgar Allan Poe* the previous year influenced Sills and Rudel to select me to compose their final New York City Opera commission. Rudel had traveled down to Baltimore to see *Poe* when it ran there. I spoke with him after the performance and his comment surprised me. He said he admired the opera but felt it would go over the heads of his New York audience—this after sitting among an audience of Marylanders who had received the work rapturously! He had not come to Baltimore with an eye to presenting *Poe* in New York, as I thought, but to evaluate me before offering the commission for a new work. Nevertheless, I know he expected to get an opera somewhat along the lines of *Poe,* and Carlotta would have been fairly similar and possibly equally successful. A major New York success would certainly have continued the rising trajectory of *Masque of Angels, Postcard from Morocco,* and *Poe.*

Despite the reversal of fortune that *Miss Havisham's Fire* brought on, I'm still glad I wrote it and dismissed the Carlotta idea. I've always admired how utterly different Mozart was able to make *Don Giovanni, Così fan tutte,* and *The Magic Flute,* operas written back-to-back. Verdi did the same with *Rigoletto, Il trovatore,* and *La traviata* (as did Britten in our time), whereas with composers like Puccini and Massenet it is often difficult to distinguish one opera from another. I prefer Mozart and Verdi as models and have taken pride in trying to make each one of my operas distinct from the others. To have composed a Carlotta opera after *Poe* would have been as much a redundancy as *Madame Butterfly* after *Tosca.* (Richard Strauss said, "*Bohème, Butterfly, Tosca,* I can't tell them apart!") *Miss Havisham,* in spite of the failure of that first version, was a worthier successor to *Poe.*

A Thanksgiving to God,
for His House
(1979)

∽

Anthem for unaccompanied chorus
4 minutes
Poetry by Robert Herrick
Performed 6 May 1979, Plymouth Congregational Church,
     Minneapolis, Minnesota; Philip Brunelle, conductor,
     Plymouth Music Series Festival Choir

I found this Herrick poem charmingly appropriate for the occasion it had been commissoned to celebrate: Philip Brunelle requested a choral piece to commemorate his anniversary at the church where he held the position of organist and choirmaster and also organized a very successful music series. Like most of the anthems I have written for the Plymouth Congregational Church choir, it was a gift. Apart from the day or two I spent composing this work after the fiasco at New York City Opera in March, much of the remainder of that year was spent attempting to salvage *Miss Havisham's Fire.* The opera, I had thought (as did many of my friends), was going to be the making of me, the zenith of my career. The fact that I devoted many months to trying to save the work is a clear indication of just how devastating the blow had been.

At first—and rather pathetically—I assigned the failure to any-thing except the opera itself. Had Beverly Sills not had the recurrence of cancer that forced her to withdraw only a few months before the premiere, things would have been very different. (She had told me of her illness and her severely weakened stamina and asked that I not say anything about it because she did not want her condition to be made public.) Rumors that she withdrew because of her dissatisfac-tion with the score circulated, of course, and no doubt influenced some attitudes. Worse still, Julius Rudel decided that at this late date one soprano alone could never prepare the encyclopedic role (Sills had asked me to write her a role that would "leave me feeling like a wrung-out rag"), so two different sopranos were needed to replace her: the younger one sang act 1 and the other act 2. Both were fine singers, but it would be difficult to find two more dissimilar voices and personalities; as a result, whatever sympathy young Miss Havisham aroused with listeners in the first act simply did not carry over for the older Miss Havisham in the second act, since she appeared to be a totally different character. Splitting the role that way eviscerated the opera: much of the work's interest was to have been in seeing an operatic superstar in an immense tour de force, going from jilted young bride to demented old lady, and concluding with the longest mad scene ever composed.

I also looked for a villain in the staging: the inquest setting—with tables, chairs, coroner, witnesses—that came and went frequently throughout the opera was placed on a large platform that was wheeled on and off as needed. Its tires squealed and the floorboards groaned. (At rehearsals we had dubbed it the Toonerville Trolley.) After its first appearance, the audience greeted each new entrance with laughter. The set itself was not exempted: the huge stage of the State Theater was a single, enormous room, three or four stories high. I had imagined two small, claustrophobic rooms. But finally, the truth had to be faced: it was the opera itself that was flawed, and even had Sills been able to perform it perfectly, the work was too long and unfocused. I spent the summer of 1979 in Florence with blue pencil, scissors, clear adhesive tape, scores, tapes of the opera's broadcast, and a tape recorder. I was determined to discover the faults and root them out: I tried rearranging scenes, omitting scenes, shortening others, convinced there had to be a magic combination or realignment that would solve the problem. But all it did was make me feel as I did with *Bravo Mozart!*—as hopelessly entangled as Laocoön. From time to time I'd take the score out and look it over sadly, then put it away again. Only after more than fifteen years had passed did I feel I had gained enough objectivity to deal with it.

Let All the World
in Every Corner Sing
(1980)

∞

Festive hymn for chorus, brass quartet, timpani, and organ
3 minutes
Poetry by George Herbert
Performed June 1980, Central Lutheran Church, Minneapolis,
   Minnesota; American Guild of Organists

The American Guild of Organists held its convention in Minneapolis in 1980, and I was asked to compose a suitable piece for the inaugurating worship service. Since the music had been completed well in advance of the event, Boosey was able to have it in print by the time the convention opened. As a result, the twenty-five hundred registered organists and choirmasters who filed into Central Lutheran Church (then the fourth largest church in the United States) that Sunday morning each received a complimentary copy of the choral score.

The first performance of the piece followed the opening prayer and welcome. It was the most remarkable premiere my music has ever had (being completely unrehearsed, among other things), and it made me appreciate what Berlioz found so exciting in creating those gigantic compositions calling for extraordinary musical forces and designed for performance in huge spaces. It is difficult for me to think of any musical event I have ever experienced that was more thrilling than hearing my music, sung by twenty-five hundred voices accompanied by brass quartet, timpani, and organ at full throttle, reverberating throughout that cathedral-like vastness. The hymn was repeated once more before the service proceeded and sounded even better this time now that the congregation was no longer sight-reading the music (naturally, the brass quartet, timpanist, and organist had looked at their parts beforehand). It is the most festive piece I have ever written and is primarily performed in churches, particularly around the Easter season.

This would be the place, I suppose, to register my grievance against the organ—the one instrument I have always been reluctant to employ. The primary reason no doubt stems from my ignorance of the instrument: its stops, mixtures, pedal technique, manuals, and so forth. These matters, I'm sure, could probably have been mastered had my antipathy not worked against it, but my dislike of virtually all organ music composed during the past century and a half—usually French, from Widor through Franck and on up to Messiaen—is very strong. It is so noisy and bombastic much of the time, exulting in its overwhelming mechanical power.

Most annoying, however, is the fact that the monster never breathes. There is a link in my mind between the phraseology—the very syntax—of music and the amount of breath expended in singing. This stems, as I theorized earlier, from my conviction that music originated in the human throat, and I think the four- or eight-measure phrase structure that prevailed in music for so long came about because it was a comfortable amount to sing before the necessity of breathing forced a caesura. That pause for an intake of air that singers cannot but observe several times a minute is required as well of all brass and woodwind players. And even though the sound produced by stringed instruments does not rely on breathing, they emulate a similar break through changes in the up-and-down movement of the bow. It is this organization of pitches into breath-sized units that gives so much of music the illusion of having a grammar, not unlike language.

Without phrasing music would be gibberish. Only percussion and keyboard instruments can ignore these actual or implied caesuras between groups of notes. And of them all, the organ is the chief offender. Its inexhaustible and effortless supply of wind is apparently too great a temptation to resist, particularly for late nineteenth- and twentieth-century organ composers. Perhaps it is the use of electrical power to produce wind that encourages this endless, inarticulate stream of sound. (I am always reminded of those bad Italian tenors who sustain high notes as though they were aspiring to the Guinness Book of World Records.) And it may be that Bach and Handel, mindful of the poor boy who had to pump the bellows, wrote more humanely for the instrument.

I have written only three pieces for solo organ. Two were gifts (processionals for the weddings of Philip Brunelle's sons), and I have not let them be published. Only the third, *Prelude for Easter's Dawning,* is published, and I later turned it into an orchestral work that sounds better—and I am far happier with it in that form.

Miss Havisham's Wedding Night (1981)

∾

Monodrama in one act
30 minutes
Libretto by John Olon-Scrymgeour, based on the character from
 Great Expectations by Charles Dickens
Performed 1 May 1981, Tyrone Guthrie Theater, Minneapolis,
 Minnesota; Rita Shane, soprano; Philip Brunelle, conduc-
 tor, Minnesota Opera

The libretto of this monodrama existed before *Miss Havisham's Fire* was composed, and not only did it provide the impetus for the commissioning of the full-length opera (via Ms. Sills's enthusiasm for the character); it also served in a somewhat abbreviated form as its epilogue. After a long struggle to redeem the failed work, I had to accept the fact that it seemed a hopeless aspiration. The opera's epilogue, however, had been conceived from the start as an independent piece and it could be rescued, I believed, although the big orchestra employed in *Miss Havisham's Fire* would be far too large and needlessly expensive for an intimate, one-character, thirty-minute piece. I reinstated the dozens of lines that had been deleted in transforming the monodrama into an epilogue, composed music for this new text, and then orchestrated the fully restored monodrama for a chamber orchestra of sixteen instruments.

The monodrama proved very effective in the theater and provided a small portion of consolation for what had been lost, rather like retrieving and preserving a single lifeboat from the *Titanic*. There was also an unanticipated benefit: *Miss Havisham's Wedding Night* became the perfect companion piece for *A Water Bird Talk,* and they are frequently double-billed. The former is for soprano, the latter for baritone; the orchestras are almost identical; and both monodramas deal with marriage—in one, a marriage that never occurred but left the jilted bride wearing a wedding gown for the remainder of her life; in the other, a marriage that did take place to the husband's enduring regret and despair.

I wish I had written more monodramas: the form is a fascinating one, challenging and fulfilling. In a way, some of my song cycles come close to becoming monodramas: *The Diary of Virginia Woolf,* certainly, *Miss Manners on Music,* perhaps, and *A Few Words about Chekhov,* but only if one can imagine a monodrama with two characters, each unaware of the other. *The Andrée Expedition* might also qualify, for although three different speakers are implied, as in Schubert's "The Erlking," a single voice carries the burden of the drama. The most moving arias in opera have usually been soliloquies; which is to say, they are operatic monologues not addressed to any other individual even though others may be present on stage: Orfeo's "Tu se' morta," Donna Elvira's "Mi tradì," Iago's "Credo," the Marschallin's "Monologue," Tosca's "Vissi d'arte," Peter Grimes's "Now the Great Bear." That is so, I believe, because soliloquies deal almost exclusively with feelings and emotions; a soul is being unburdened. Operatic monologues that are addressed to another character most often deal with facts or information, and facts or information are less at home in music than emotions and feelings. One of opera's greatest characters, Don Giovanni, has only one tiny aria to sing, "Fin ch'han dal vino." But that is not so surprising considering that the Don is a doer, not a thinker; he requires no big arias because he is never disturbed by conscience or introspection.

A monodrama, as I see it, is basically a chain of soliloquies (as are some of the song cycle texts cited above). They are grist for music's mill since one of the most challenging and fruitful aspects of opera is the possibility it provides the composer of creating character through music. That characterization is more likely to take place in arias—where revelation or confession more readily occurs—than in recitatives, where more mundane matters are explored. In a full-length opera's two or three hours' duration, characters rarely have more than three arias. Embedded in the far shorter *Miss Havisham's Wedding Night* and in *A Water Bird Talk* are at least six arias, although their boundaries are not always distinct.

Peter Quince at the Clavier
(1981)

∾

Sonatina for mixed chorus and piano concertante
20 minutes
Poetry by Wallace Stevens
Performed 11 April 1981, Schwab Auditorium, Pennsylvania State
    University, College Park, Pennsylvania; Raymond Brown,
    conductor, Penn State Singers

*P**eter Quince at the Clavier* was commissioned
by Pennsylvania State University to
celebrate the tercentenary of the State of Pennsylvania. I was chosen
because I was born in Pennsylvania. It seemed a point of honor with
the commissioners, understandably, that the words of the new composition should also be by a native of the state. My research into early or
historical texts that might satisfy the commissioners as Pennsylvanians
and at the same time interest me as a composer yielded very little apart
from some uninspiring bucolic prose by William Penn (after whom
my high school in York had been named) and a very brief flirtation
with Benjamin Franklin in his humorous vein, neither of which
was likely to awaken my muse. That left contemporary poetry, which
I knew would be a more productive area to explore. I had become
reluctant to set modern poems because (1) obtaining the copyright

owner's permission was often problematic and, more important, (2) the obfuscation of much modern poetry turns hopelessly dense when slowed down and stretched out, as must happen when it is set to music. A complex thought or image is fine when one has time to pause and contemplate it or to back up and go over it again. Music by its very nature is always ongoing, pulling one forward, and doesn't allow time to stop and reexamine or dissect the phrase that has just been played or to linger over a felicitous sound.

An exception to these points, however, must be made for the poetry I used for my opus I, *Songs about Spring.* In the case of e e cummings, the poet and his publishers have always seemed willing to grant permission to composers seeking to use his poems in songs and choral pieces. Furthermore, both his language and images are generally quite simple and not infrequently childlike. As a matter of fact, since most musical settings of cummings's poems tend to disregard the typographical oddities of the page, their meaning is often more easily apprehended when sung than when read. And on the contrary, composers who have attempted to create an aural substitute for cummings's eccentric visual layout (injecting sudden pauses, musical non sequiturs, and the like) have ended up making some poems virtually incomprehensible. I suspect it is my disinclination to set modern poetry that has so often prompted me to select letters and diaries instead.

The choice of text in this case was quickly narrowed down to the poems of Wallace Stevens, born in Reading, Pennsylvania. And while I can't claim to understand thoroughly everything about "Peter Quince at the Clavier" (for instance, why is a rustic from a Shakespeare play sitting at the clavier?), I found the colors, images, and words incredibly rich and beautiful ("Music is feeling, then, not sound"), and I wholeheartedly agree with those who are more knowledgeable than I that "Peter Quince" is perhaps the finest poem written by an American. I also believe it must be credited with inspiring the production of one of my best scores. I was strongly tempted, after the enjoyment I derived from setting this Stevens text, to go on and tackle his "Sunday Morning." It, too, is not entirely clear in my mind, but, like "Peter Quince," enough of it comes through and moves me profoundly that I'm sure it would have spurred me on to a better-than-average score as well.

Why didn't I do it? There is an old vaudeville adage: never follow a banjo act with a banjo act. By the time the reader gets to the end of this catalogue, I hope it will be apparent that the dozen or so operas I have composed represent an earnest effort to avoid any formulaic approach from one to another. My attitude has always been "the next one will be different," and it applies to song cycles and choral works as well. Even short anthems or motets—far less amenable to being distinctive—fall under this rubric.

Fire Variations
(1982)

❦

Eight variations and a finale based on a blacksmith's work song
20 minutes
Performed 24 April 1982, Concordia College, Moorhead,
    Minnesota; J. Robert Hanson, conductor, Fargo-
    Moorhead Symphony Orchestra

The monodrama that blossomed out of the epilogue to *Miss Havisham's Fire* was an attempt to lessen the disappointment of that experience. *Fire Variations* was similarly motivated. It had been commissioned by the Fargo-Moorhead Symphony, and I agreed to do it mainly because I had written nothing for orchestra since 1977 and the field of opera was still looking unattractive to me.

In *Great Expectations* Pip sings a work song he learned at the forge while helping Joe Gargery and the other blacksmiths. Dickens supplied the lyrics for "Old Clem," which I had assumed was a genuine work song known by the author. (That Saint Clement actually is the patron saint of blacksmiths gave it a verifying touch.) But inquiries to the Dickens Society in London and to other sources failed to uncover a single note of its tune. Consequently, the work song Pip sings in the opera is my own invention, and I decided to use its simple melody as a theme for a set of variations.

Variation form is a favorite of mine; *The Mask of Night*, the mono-drama *A Water Bird Talk, A Toccata of Galuppi's,* and *Reverie* are also cast as sets of variations. One of the classic examples of the form is Brahms's *Variations on a Theme by Haydn.* Restudying the Brahms score, a scheme began to form for my own piece: with a tune I associated with black-smiths, each variation of Pip's tune would take its cue from different fire images—smoldering, blazing, cozy, threatening, and so on—and, at the same time, each one would be a variation on one of Brahms's own variations, matching measure for measure, tempo for tempo, compositional techniques, orchestration dynamics, and so on. In effect, the work would become a set of double variations. Those who knew Brahms's piece well would easily spot the connection between his variations and mine; those who did not, could take the work at face value—as a simple set of variations.

As was the case with *In Praise of Music,* Boosey & Hawkes submitted *Fire Variations* for the Friedheim Award. This time it not only qualified but was one of the five finalists. These five pieces were presented in a Sunday afternoon concert at the Kennedy Center. I knew two of the finalists personally: David Del Tredici, a well-established composer, and Gundaris Ponè, who had been a student at the University of Minnesota when I first arrived in Minneapolis. The remaining two were unknown to me: one, a woman regarded primarily as a guitarist, I believe, and the other, a local (Washington, D.C.) composer none of us had ever heard of and whose composition (evidently the antithe-sis of the Auden-Bernstein *Age of Anxiety*) was titled *The Age of Victory.* At the end of the concert the judges retired to deliberate. When they returned, David (I expected he would place first) was awarded third prize. Gundaris (I thought he would place third) was given second prize. I held my breath, since the music of the two unknowns had made little impression on me and who else was left? Then the announce-ment: "The first prize goes . . . [I was buttoning my jacket, preparing to go up onstage] . . . to the composer from Washington!" I have never again heard his name or music.

With the exception of the *Haydn Variations,* Brahms's music does very little for me. I have a blind spot where he is concerned, and I realize that very few of my peers share this antipathy. He is undeniably a wonderful technician, a consummate master. However, if there is such a thing as being too well made, that is how his art strikes me. His symphonies have been smoothed, refined, and burnished to a fare-thee-well, and it has been done at the cost of spontaneity and freshness (someone once said his music stinks of the studio). His perfection (which I grant he achieves constantly) seems stolid, labored, and studied, unlike the perfection of Mozart, which in contrast feels almost casual, graceful, and effortless.

I Hate and I Love
(Odi et Amo)
(1982)

∞

Cycle for mixed chorus and percussion
15 minutes
Poetry by Gaius Catullus
Performed 14 March 1982, Orchestra Hall, Minneapolis,
    Minnesota; Dale Warland, conductor, Dale Warland
    Singers

This is the first piece the Dale Warland Singers commissioned from me, although I was familiar with Dale's fine work a dozen years earlier, when he premiered *Tria Carmina Paschalia,* and from other concerts I had attended in the years since. In my opinion this has been Minnesota's premier choral group deserving national as well as regional attention. I have yet to meet a choral conductor who can match the results he invariably obtains: a comparison of Dale's recording of this work with the one made by Robert Shaw, the man generally regarded as America's finest choral conductor, will easily confirm my opinion and Dale's superiority.

I Hate and I Love was composed during the summer in Florence. During rest periods I had been reading the poetry of Catullus (in Salvatore Quasimodo's Italian translation), and although I had something quite different in mind for use as text for Dale's piece, I was struck by the idea of composing a set of pieces that mixed hot and cold feelings as Catullus's own work does. I selected six poems and translated them into English (cribbing from Quasimodo's version, which was printed on facing pages).

The poem of the title serves as both the first and last piece, suggesting that the love-hate cycle is about to be repeated, perhaps endlessly. The five poems in between are arranged in contrasting order. For the accompanying instruments (it had been requested that I use only a few), and considering the antiquity of the text and the emotions, I decided against piano, strings, woodwinds, or brass, opting for something less time-specific: percussion. Seen from this distance, my penchant for *la batteria* (the Italian term is much more colorful) is readily noted as their prominence in this choral work, *The Revelation of Saint John the Divine,* and *Jonah and the Whale* makes obvious and as the subtitle of *A Ring of Time* attests.

In the first quarter century covered by this catalogue, just four choral works are listed, the first only appearing some sixteen years after opus I. In the concluding quarter century there are twelve. Some of this imbalance is explained by commissions, which have been far more prevalent in the latter period. In the former period, when commissions were scarcer, I was frequently free to choose what to write and only once—in *A Nation of Cowslips*—did I write for chorus by choice. This was probably because I had never sung in a group. The music courses I had to take during junior high school were little more than fifty-minute sessions of excruciating boredom occasioned by those awful paperbound anthologies (*America Sings* and *55*) containing such gems as "Reuben, Reuben, I've Been Thinking," "Little Brown Jug," and "The Church in the Wildwood." I sat at the rear of the class, lips firmly sealed, surreptitiously drawing war planes in flames on the music's margins while Mrs. Fink enthusiastically waved her arms about with little regard to tempo.

My aversion to vocal music in general persisted into my third year at Peabody (where I avoided taking chorus entirely). Study with Hugo Weisgall and marriage to a soprano spurred my new interest in opera and song, but it took a much longer time for me to develop an appreciation of group singing. No doubt, living in Minnesota had a considerable hand in fostering it. Later, concern for using the most appropriate vocal medium—singular or plural—for a particular text also prompted my increasing involvement with choruses. For example, although *I Hate and I Love* is in the first person, I felt it had to be sung by a chorus. I'd never dream of giving it to a solo voice; I think it would be unseemly.

Over the years, unbeknownst to me, an idiosyncrasy has developed: when writing for chorus I have tended to select poetry, the Bible, liturgy (i.e., words written for public discourse), but when writing for solo voice I have preferred the use of prose—letters, diaries, and other words written for private discourse. The distinction "public versus private," not "we versus I," usually governed whether a selected text would become a work for chorus or a work for solo voice.

The Andrée Expedition
(1982)

∾

Thirteen songs for baritone and piano
40 minutes
Journals and letters of Salomon Andrée, Nils Strindberg, and
    Knut Frankel
Performed 15 February 1983, O'Shaughnessy Auditorium, Saint
    Paul, Minnesota; Håkan Hagegård, baritone; Thomas
    Schuback, piano

With its thirteen songs, *The Andrée Expedition* is the most ambitious of my song cycles, although in duration it is only five or six minutes longer than the *Woolf* cycle's eight diary excerpts. It was commissioned by the Schubert Club and written with a specific singer in mind, the popular Swedish baritone Håkan Hagegård, and the personality of the singer determined the choice of text.

On a Saturday morning during one of my traditional forays into the university library, I was searching for a suitable text for this work. I had nothing specific in mind, but having drifted away from the literature stacks, I found myself wandering among categories I had never visited before. A title caught my eye: *The Flight of the Eagle.* Taking it down, I saw that it was a translation from Swedish of the true story of a nineteenth-century Swedish balloonist, Salomon Andrée. When I was a boy, my favorite hobby had been building model airplanes, and I dreamed of becoming what was then called an "aviator." My interest was immediately aroused by a glance through the book. I looked up other books related to Andrée's expedition to the North Pole and checked them all out.

The subject itself at first got my attention, not the idea of using the material for a cycle. That came later, after absorbing more of the available facts and speculating about the possibilities. Naturally the Swedish connection played a part in persuading me to find a way to make the history into a musical work. Schubert's "Erlking"—which I heard Hagegård perform in recital around this time—provided the idea of asking a single singer to impersonate the three characters who went on the expedition. The texts for Andrée and Strindberg were taken directly (and edited) from their diaries and letters. Frankel's journal contained only technical data about the flight—nothing I could use for song. Consequently, I took advantage of his "reticence" and invented a text that was partly gleaned from Frankel's two companions and partly of my own contrivance in order to express a point of view about the men and their courageous but doomed undertaking.

Originally, two similar characters of dissimilar nationalities competed to become the basic material of this song cycle. In the end, preference was given to Andrée, with Hagegård's nationality tipping the balance. But making a decision was both difficult—since I found the two equally engrossing—and regrettable because owing to certain similarities, using one meant dismissing the other from any future consideration. Had the singer I had in mind been Spanish or Latin American, the choice might well have gone the other way.

Andrée had a fascinating rival in Alberto Santos-Dumont, a Brazilian millionaire and flamboyant playboy. His book, *My Airships,* gives a delightful account of his experiments with balloons, dirigibles, and, later in his career, heavier-than-air craft. They were often seen over Paris, where he would frequently touch down at a café for refreshments, his servants running through the streets below him in order to tether the balloon while their master snacked or imbibed. Santos-Dumont was the first man to succeed, repeatedly, in leaving the ground, flying through the air to a place of his own choosing, and landing safely. He often invited friends to enjoy picnics in his balloon. A genuine eccentric, he had his dining room table and chairs suspended from the ceiling, several meters above the floor, so that he could—as he said—get used to eating in the air.

There was a serious side to him as well: he entered and sometimes won important competitions with airships of his own invention and had numerous hair-raising scrapes with death while navigating the air. In 1910 came tragedy: an incurable disease forced him to give up flying. He returned to Brazil and slowly descended into madness. He ended his life by committing suicide, blaming himself for all the sorrows and ills (aerial bombing, air crashes, disasters) that his invention had brought to humankind. He never acknowledged, or remained ignorant of, the attribution of "his" invention to the Wright brothers. A wonderful song cycle might have come of all this had not its similarity to *Andrée* pushed it off-limits.

Two weeks before the premiere of *Andrée,* Håkan phoned Bruce Carlson at the Schubert Club, said that the cycle was really very demanding, and asked if it would be all right to perform just six or seven of the thirteen songs. With Swede-to-Swede bluntness, Bruce said no, it would not be all right. A week later Håkan called again: it was such a difficult work—perhaps he could sing seven or eight of the songs and *recite* the texts of the others. No. A compromise: if Håkan and his pianist would work with the composer the day before the concert, they could decide together which songs would or would not be performed.

Håkan and his accompanist, Thomas Schuback, arrived at my house at 10 a.m. the day before the premiere. We worked diligently, song by song. Being the superb musicians they are, the few inaccuracies and uncertainties were quickly eliminated and the first half of the cycle was in pretty good shape by noon. After a relaxing lunch, their confidence and enthusiasm growing by the minute, we cleaned up the second half and by 4 that afternoon we all agreed there was no need to omit anything at all. Carolyn suggested tea and they happily accepted, relishing the relief they were now feeling.

Håkan asked if I had a recording of Janet Baker doing the *Woolf* cycle, a work he knew she had premiered but had never heard. I told them there was a tape of the rehearsal and I played it while we had our tea. As the piece was ending, I noticed that Håkan and Thomas were noticeably subdued, misty-eyed. I was wondering if their reaction was a tribute to Janet's exquisite artistry or to the work when Håkan spoke up: "We are so ashamed. She comes to rehearsal and gives a perfect performance while we had hoped you'd settle for half a performance." The apology wasn't necessary: the next night they redeemed themselves giving the work a splendid premiere.

Prelude for Easter Dawning
(1982)

∞

Organ solo
5 minutes
Performed Easter Sunday 1982, Plymouth Congregational
   Church, Minneapolis, Minnesota; Philip Brunelle, organist

This is yet another composition prompted by a request from Philip Brunelle. In lieu of a commission, *Prelude for Easter Dawning* was written on the assurance that the work would be included in a soon-to-be-published anthology of contemporary organ music to be issued by Oxford University Press. That was less my reason for writing the piece than my friendship with Philip, who over the years had been a truly committed champion of my music. Since he intended to perform the piece as a prelude for Easter morning worship service, several thoughts occurred to me: the music should attempt to suggest a dawning, something beginning in full darkness and gradually growing brighter and brighter like a rising sun; then, at its peak, the music should evolve into my favorite Easter hymn, "Ellacombe," played with the full power of the instrument. I had hoped that it could be arranged for the congregation to arise at the end and sing the hymn through in the usual fashion, which is precisely what happened at the first performance I attended.

I am unable to judge how idiomatic the piece may be. I have received mail from organists pointing out various solecisms, the worst offense evidently (since it was cited by several writers) being slurs in a pedal part requiring the left foot to sustain one note while the right foot was asked to slur from one note to another a sixth above. Even in my ignorance I knew that the two notes could not actually be slurred; a slight break would have to occur. I had simply used a slur marking to connect the two notes in order to identify the figure as one of the piece's principal motives. One writer complimented me on the piece and asked whether I might have other works for the instrument and/or would be interested in accepting a commission for a new piece. I replied that I was not interested, and as this catalogue makes plain, I was never tempted to write a similar piece again. This composition for solo organ remains *solus.*

The piece remains *solus* in another sense: it is the only work of mine that was not originally published by Boosey & Hawkes, although sometime after the Oxford University Press anthology appeared Boosey published *Prelude* as a separate item. My association with Boosey—the only publisher I've ever had—was initiated in 1957 and is just a few years short of having endured half a century. That may or may not be some sort of record. (All the big-name twentieth-century composers that Boosey handled at one time—notably Stravinsky, Bartók, Strauss, Britten, Copland—had other publishers before or after having been with B & H.) When I signed with them, Stuart Pope, only recently promoted to New York from the Cape Town office, was the president, a position he would hold for three decades or more. I think he genuinely enjoyed my music, particularly the choral things since his musical background seems to have been church-related, organ and choir primarily. He and his wife, Doris, made numerous trips to Minneapolis, attending virtually every premiere

I ever had—here and elsewhere—during his tenure. A close friendship developed, and for a good many years the two of them would
spend a week or so each summer as our guests in the apartment at via
dei Bardi 58. I must confess that my relationship with the publishing
house, though it continues to this day, has not remained as warm as
it had been before Stuart retired. His leaving is the principal reason
for the detachment I now feel, and the much briefer tenures of his
various successors—four so far—and my lack of familiarity with them
has also contributed to that condition.

Casa Guidi
(1983)

∾

Five songs for mezzo-soprano and orchestra
22 minutes
Letters of Elizabeth Barrett Browning to her sister Henrietta
Performed 28 September 1983, Orchestra Hall, Minneapolis,
    Minnesota; Frederica von Stade, mezzo; Neville Marriner,
    conductor, Minnesota Orchestra

Neville Marriner wanted to commission a work for Janet Baker and the Minnesota Orchestra, but at that time she was curtailing her appearances in the United States. One afternoon I sat in Neville's office while he phoned Frederica von Stade. He asked if she was interested in having a new work written for her. She was. He handed me the phone and, after introducing myself, I asked if there was any special poetry or poet she'd prefer.

Her first choice didn't surprise me: Robert Frost. I think of Frost as a boy's poet, and Frederica was famous for *hosenrollen* ("trousers roles"—women playing young men), especially Cherubino and Octavian. But I don't find Frost very congenial for musical treatment, and I asked for a second choice. Sylvia Plath! Now that was surprising: as I see them, she and Frederica seem to occupy two completely different wavelengths.

I decided it would be best if I chose the text for her: something feminine and vulnerable. I looked among women poets and settled on Elizabeth Barrett Browning. As was the case with Virginia Woolf, her public writings led me to look up the private writings, and I ended up choosing the latter—Elizabeth's many letters from Florence to her sister Henrietta in England. It was natural to focus on the Brownings' home: we always lived only a few blocks from Casa Guidi in Florence and had often taken our guests to visit it.

It should be mentioned here that of the half dozen or so famous singers for whom I have written, Flicka has been my favorite, and I think my fondness for the works I've composed for her is a clear reflection of that partiality. In addition to *Casa Guidi,* another song cycle (*A Few Words about Chekhov*) and an opera (*The Aspern Papers*) were written specifically for her unique gifts, and I would have happily written more pieces had the occasion presented itself. I flatter myself (and apologize for the immodesty) in believing that a natural affinity exists between her vocal performances and my vocal compositions, for I find in her voice and sensibilities precisely those same qualities I have wished to put into my music: beauty, intelligence, genuineness, absence of showiness, humanity. (In fact, Flicka's recording of *Casa Guidi* was nominated for a 2004 Grammy for best classical vocal performance.)

Strangely enough, in reckoning the many years we have spent in Florence, *Casa Guidi* is only my third (and last) work inspired by that magnificent city: *A Ring of Time* and *The Mask of Night* preceded it. Over the years, I had considered making operas of Alfred de Musset's drama based on Alexander dei Medici, *Lorenzaccio,* a pair or trio of Boccaccio's tales, and, most attractive of all, Thomas Mann's beautiful play about Savonarola, *Fiorenza.* The city affected my music in many ways, I suppose: walking the same streets as Dante, Michelangelo, Machiavelli, Cellini, Ghirlandaio was a constant prod to aspiration, a reminder of what it was possible to achieve in the world of art; passing the palazzo where a group of intellectuals had gathered, hoping to re-create the original method of performing Greek tragedies but who wound up inventing opera instead; attending concerts in a room of the Pitti Palace where the very first opera was performed; leaving a store in via dei Neri where my visiting librettist, John, purchased a pair of shoes and looking up at the plaque above the door that identified the building as the birthplace of Ottavio Rinuccini, the first librettist; museums, churches, trattorias, the people. All these things, too, somehow placed a mark on my music.

But in truth, my love for Florence has less to do with my professional life than might be supposed. My initial acquaintance with Florence had been affected by that unhappy experience with Dallapiccola at the outset, and it muted the city's charms for much of that year. Returning five years later with a wife whose father was a Methodist minister, I was concerned how Carolyn would respond to a culture so very different from the one she had known, and thus I was not surprised that she felt ill when we stepped off the train at the Florence station. We checked into a *pensione,* where she stayed in bed for a week while I, greatly disheartened, looked for an apartment to rent for a year. (I tried to cheer her up with a gesture any of Henry James's fans would recognize: I bought her some marrons glacés at Doney's Café in via Tornabuoni; they only made her blanch.)

It turned out that Carolyn had not been sickened by Italy but had contracted influenza, which was virulent that year. After she recovered and we moved into the handsome apartment at Lungarno Torrigiani 7, her spirits quickly soared and in time she became a greater lover of Florence than I was. Since then, Florence has been the place where we have never failed to find contentment, where the two of us feel more at home than we do in Minneapolis, and where, as soon as we leave, we yearn to return. It is little wonder that I do my best work there, but that is simply because we are happier there than we are anywhere else.

Casanova's Homecoming
(1984)

∞

Opera buffa in three acts
134 minutes
Libretto by the composer based on *L'histoire de ma vie* by Jacques
    Casanova
Performed 12 April 1986, Ordway Music Theatre, Saint Paul,
    Minnesota; Julian Patrick, baritone; Suzanne Marcy,
    mezzo; Scott Bergson, conductor, Saint Paul Chamber
    Orchestra, Minnesota Opera Company

The Ordway Music Theatre was due to open in 1985, and the Minnesota Opera, one of the three groups to occupy this new home, asked me for an inaugural work. Two conditions were imposed: that it be a comedy and that I be my own librettist. "New home" in Italian is *casa nuova* (while in England, Casanova styled himself "Mr. Newhouse"), and thoughts of an opera buffa about Casanova set in Venice—a city Carolyn and I love as much as Florence—began to form. Finally being asked to compose another opera after the New York City Opera disaster felt wonderful, and the writing of both words and music left me feeling on top of the world—until a third breach of faith by the Minnesota Opera embittered me.

The first deception had occurred in 1965, when we returned from a year abroad to discover that in my absence the Walker Art

Center had chosen its own opera manager and the artistic direction of Center Opera had been changed. The second perfidy was in 1975, concerning *The Voyage of Edgar Allan Poe*. It was no secret that I composed the role of Poe's wife, Virginia, specifically for Carolyn, but someone (Charles Fullmer, manager of the opera company, Wesley Balk, the stage director, or Brunelle, the music director—I have never tried to find out which one) had other plans and gave the part to another soprano over my objection. Of course I understood that a very petite soprano would be ideal to impersonate Poe's child bride, but Carolyn was hardly a Valkyrie. Furthermore, sopranos her size and larger have been fine when the opera was done in Dallas, Chicago, Sweden, and Germany. I was sorely tempted to bar the production, but since it had been commissioned by the university in honor of the Bicentennial, I did not feel I had the right to do so.

And now the third outrage (and that's not too strong a word): Brunelle or Fullmer replaced *Casanova's Homecoming* with a Swedish musical, *Animalen,* which had been highly successful in Scandinavia, to inaugurate a new American opera house! The work proved a complete failure in Saint Paul, despite the expectation that the ethnic makeup of the area would guarantee great interest. Unfortunately, its supporters failed to take into account that the political content (antiwar), which had made it so popular in Sweden, was inimical to the gala celebratory occasion we all anticipated. I felt sorry for the talented composer, Lars-Johann Werle, whom I befriended and later visited several times in Sweden. He had been led to hope that Saint Paul might be an out-of-town tryout leading to a Broadway run. The review in *Newsweek* pretty much summed up the consensus: "Why open this new music center with a poor foreign opera when this is Argento's town?" A few months later, *Casanova* opened and was a big success. It went on to New York City Opera the following season, played to sold-out houses, and was revived the next year. It received the 1986 National Institute for Music Theater Award.

A historical footnote: Beverly Sills, then director of New York City Opera and our coproducer, was in favor of performing *Casanova* with supertitles (or surtitles, as they're often called). They had proved their worth in foreign-language operas but had not yet been employed when an opera was sung in the audience's own language—in this case, English. I objected—it was a slur on my ability to set English comprehensibly, a point I take some pride in, and I managed to convince the Minnesota Opera to reject the idea for the premiere performances here. But in Sills's own house, her will prevailed and *Casanova* became the first opera in English to have English supertitles. I will admit that when I finally saw the opera with supertitles, many more of the libretto's jokes were understood (the *New York Times* took exception to so many), and there was twice as much laughter. A benefit I had not expected: the increase in the audience's enjoyment was matched by an increase in the performers' vitality and spiritedness, adding up to a much more polished and assured performance.

Le Tombeau d'Edgar Poe
(1985)

~

Suite from the opera *The Voyage of Edgar Allan Poe*
16 minutes
Performed 27 February 1986, Meyerhoff Symphony Hall,
      Baltimore, Maryland; David Zinman, conductor,
      Baltimore Symphony

During my first year at the University of Minnesota, David Zinman was a graduate student and a teaching assistant who shared my office. It was clear from our first meeting that he was highly gifted in violin and conducting (and not quite as gifted in composing, a discipline he also enjoyed). After graduation and further study with Pierre Monteux, his blossoming career took him to Amsterdam, Rochester (New York), Baltimore, and back to Minneapolis as artistic director for several seasons of Sommerfest with the Minnesota Orchestra. While serving as conductor of the Baltimore Symphony (the orchestra I enjoyed weekly during my years at Peabody), David commissioned me. After its 1976 premiere in Saint Paul, the Poe opera was booked for a weeklong run in Baltimore, which was appropriate: Poe and his family had lived in that city for a number of years, and

Carolyn, Howard Hanson, and the Eastman–Rochester Philharmonic premiering Ode to the West Wind, *May 1957. Courtesy of the Eastman School of Music.*

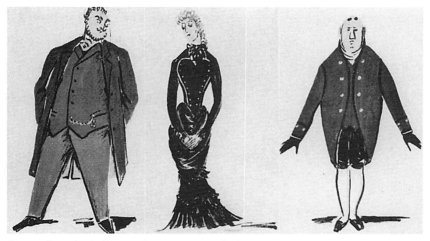

Costume design for the German television premiere of The Boor, *December 1960.*

German premiere of the ballet The Resurrection of Don Juan, *Karlsruhe Staats-theater, winter 1959.*

Librettist and director John Olon-Scrymgeour and the composer during a rehearsal of The Masque of Angels, *December 1963. Courtesy of the Minnesota Opera's Archives.*

Premiere of The Masque of Angels *at Center Opera, Guthrie Theater, 9 January 1964. Costumes by Peter Wexler. Courtesy of the Minnesota Opera's Archives.*

Carolyn preparing to perform the role of Venus for the opening of The Masque of Venus and Adonis *at Center Opera, Guthrie Theater, 9 January 1964. Costumes by Peter Wexler. Courtesy of the Minnesota Opera's Archives.*

Premiere cast of **Postcard from Morocco**, *October 1971. Setting and costume designs by Jon Barkla. Courtesy of the Minnesota Opera's Archives.*

The composer in Florence during the composition of **A Ring of Time**. *Photograph by Carolyn Bailey.*

Neville Marriner and the composer reviewing Casa Guidi *before the Carnegie Hall premiere, February 1984. Courtesy of the Minnesota Orchestra.*

Frederica von Stade and the composer rehearsing for the premiere of Casa Guidi, *September 1983. Courtesy of the Minnesota Orchestra.*

The composer and Dame Janet Baker after the Carnegie Hall pre-miere of From the Diary of Virginia Woolf, *December 1975.*

Cast in the Dallas Opera's premiere of The Aspern Papers, *19 November 1988. Photograph by Phil Schexnyder. Courtesy of the Dallas Opera.*

Wesley H. Balk, director, the composer, and Beverly Sills, discussing New York City Opera's staging of Miss Havisham's Fire *in 1979.*

Soprano Erie Mills in the title role of Miss Havisham's Fire *at the Opera Theatre of Saint Louis. Photograph copyright 2001 Ken Howard. Reprinted with permission.*

Poster for premiere of Casanova's Homecoming *at the Ordway Music Theatre, Saint Paul, Minnesota, April 1986. Courtesy of the Minnesota Opera's Archives.*

Carolyn and the composer at Florian's, Casanova's favorite café in the Piazza San Marco, Venice. Photograph by Ann Zelle.

he died and was buried there. I took advantage of the run to visit Poe's tiny home (where he wrote "Annabel Lee") and the old church graveyard where his tomb is located.

Thinking about a new piece for Baltimore I kept coming back to something relating to Poe or his poetry. Almost a decade had passed since the opera had last been performed, and arranging a suite of its music seemed a practical idea, although the form of a simple suite didn't seem interesting enough. I devised a plan to give the piece greater shape and coherence: from time to time an offstage tenor would be heard singing stanzas of "Annabel Lee" (in the opera it had been set as a nineteenth-century parlor song) while the orchestra at first accompanies him and then continues alone, elaborating on it and other music from the opera. David told me that Mr. Meyerhoff, the man who paid for the commission, was furious when he heard that I had composed a suite from my own opera. "Used goods!" he protested. However, after the premiere he generously admitted that he was thoroughly happy with the music, despite its tainted origins. I was told that he rarely had much praise for the many pieces he had commissioned.

Thinking about this work and the return to Baltimore for its premiere brought back to mind many pleasant memories of that city, and while the comparison of Peabody to Eastman as institutions leaves the former wanting, Baltimore as a place to live was more enjoyable for me than Rochester. Part of it, certainly, was due to personal circumstances: in one city I was a bachelor, in the other a husband; in one I lived in a noisy boardinghouse with a dozen pianos and other instruments producing a continual (and pleasurable) cacophony, in the other I lived in an apartment in someone else's home where not even a radio disturbed the silence; in one, my hometown was but an hour's drive away and weekend visits were frequent, while the other was a seven-hour drive, which meant a single visit during the Christmas holidays (perhaps) and summer (usually). Weather was another major factor. Baltimore had steamy summers but pleasant winters; in a Rochester winter, there were icy blasts off Lake Ontario that could easily challenge the worst Minnesota has to offer. Citizens, too, were different: Baltimoreans are truly southerners—laid back, gentle, and courteous; Rochester, because of its contented and well-paid workforce (Kodak, Bausch & Lomb, etc.), had earned the sobriquet "Smug Town USA"). But mostly, I think my fond memories of Baltimore have to do with the camaraderie of fellow students—Pete DeLone, Jack Hutton, Al Rosenthal, Tommy Newsome, Wally Kramer—all of us crowded into a booth at the neighborhood grill from 11 p.m. to 1 a.m. every evening, bottles of Budweiser, liverwurst sandwiches, and endless discussions about music, old and new, good and bad. Without question, I was much happier and more fulfilled professionally at Rochester, but it was in Baltimore that I felt wonderfully carefree and enjoyed sociability, joyfulness, and fun. Or am I merely confusing that with youth?

Capriccio for
Clarinet and Orchestra
(1985)

∾

Concerto for clarinet
24 minutes
Movement titles taken from Gioacchino Rossini's *Sins of My Old Age*
Performed 16 May 1986, Powell Hall, Saint Louis, Missouri;
    George Silfies, clarinet; Leonard Slatkin, conductor,
    Saint Louis Symphony Orchestra

The clarinet was the instrument in which I minored, one of the requirements for a master's degree at Peabody. I only studied—and rented—
the clarinet for one year but had a fine teacher, the first chair of
the Baltimore Symphony (and later of the National Symphony in
Washington, D.C.), Sidney Forrest. I enjoyed the clarinet so much
that my progress was fairly rapid, and by the end of that year I was
playing a Stamitz concerto and Hindemith sonata. Sidney encouraged me to continue my studies after I met the minor requirement,
and I've often wished that I had. Even though I became a clarinetist manqué in his eyes, Sidney continued to take an interest in my
career as a composer over the years, showing up anytime something
of mine was performed in the Baltimore—Washington area.

The *Capriccio* was a commission from the Saint Louis Symphony for their first-chair player, George Silfies. During my undergraduate years at Peabody, George was a teacher of keyboard harmony and a fine accompanist, dating and eventually marrying Sue Thomas, a piano major and one of Carolyn's best friends. The title "concerto" (and the piece really is a concerto) was deliberately avoided out of respect for—and intimidation by—Mozart's Clarinet Concerto, whose slow movement is, for me, one of the supremely beautiful moments in all of music. The lighthearted tone of the *Capriccio* was also an effort to eschew any comparison with Mozart's masterpiece. The work's subtitle, *Rossini in Paris,* came about because it was my first commission to compose a virtuosic piece for solo instrument and orchestra and that brought to mind Paganini's commission to Berlioz that resulted in *Harold in Italy.* Originally I had thought of taking themes from Rossini's *Sins of My Old Age,* but since that had been done before by Respighi, Britten, and others, I opted instead to take only the whimsical titles of three of his piano pieces as points of departure for the three movements of the *Capriccio.* Unfortunately, the full implication of the humor in those titles isn't usually apparent to the listener— nor, for that matter, do they need to be—but they were useful to me in composing and may be worth explaining here.

The first movement, *Une réjouissance,* refers to Rossini's first prolonged stay in Paris, when he produced a string of operatic triumphs culminating in *William Tell* and was the most popular figure of his time in that city. The middle movement, *Une caresse à ma femme,* was Rossini's own loving tribute to his second wife, Olympe Pélissier, who nursed him throughout the many years of illness that followed his retirement from the operatic world. At the heart of this movement, the clarinet part is marked *con licenza, quasi un duetto in recit.,* with music like a conversation between the high and low registers of the instrument and intended to suggest an exchange of vows—*t'amo.* The finale, *Un petit train du plaisir,* is an allusion to the famous Saturday night parties given by the Rossinis after his recovery, invitations to which were coveted by every celebrated visitor to Paris. During these *soirées musicales,* Rossini himself performed many of the *Sins of My Old Age* for the first time. *Un petit train* must have had a hilarious reception from the guests when Rossini presented it. His horror of the newfangled railway travel was well known (he fainted from fright on his first and only train ride): the printed score includes text at appropriate spots describing, among other things, the accelerating speed, the train wreck, and, finally, the angels collecting the souls of the dead passengers. The most significant influence on my score, however, comes less from Rossini's delightful music or humor than from his philosophy: that all works of art do not need to aspire to transcendence—sometimes entertainment is quite enough.

This would be a good place to say a few words about the Argento curse. I would estimate that two out of every three occasions when I've had to acknowledge an audience's applause have ended in some gaffe, faux pas, or outright disaster. The light that failed at my New York Philharmonic debut has already been cited. At Carnegie Hall, I made a special point of checking the location of steps to the stage before the concert began. When Neville and Flicka finished *Casa Guidi,* they waved to me to join them onstage. Arriving at the spot where I knew the steps should be, I no longer saw them there—I think they might have been retractable. In any case, I had to walk to the center front of the first row of seats and stand on tiptoe while Flicka got down on her knees so that we could at least clasp hands. At a premiere in a cathedral, I sat throughout the performance with my jacket unbuttoned. As soon as the applause started, I quickly and surreptitiously buttoned up as I rose and started walking toward the altar. From the titters and gasps that accompanied my progress I soon became aware that I had put the top button in the bottom buttonhole, providing a good impression of Quasimodo on his way to the bell tower.

But the worst of them all happened in connection with the *Capriccio.* At rehearsal I was shown a seat at the end on an aisle at the far side of the hall. A few feet away was a side door that led into a dark corridor at the end of which was another door opening onto the backstage area. As soon as my piece ended I was to head backstage and wait in the wings for the conductor, Leonard Slatkin, to bring me onstage. The piece ended, I quickly rose and exited into the dark corridor, went to what I thought was the second door and hurried through it—only to find myself on the sidewalk and then hear the door clang shut behind me. Naturally, it could not be opened from the outside. I raced around the building looking for a stage door entrance, found it, took a minute to convince the doorman I was who I said I was, and reached the wings just as the applause was dying away.

Te Deum
(Verba Domini Cum Verbis Populi)
(1987)

∞

Oratorio for chorus and orchestra
42 minutes
Te Deum (Latin) and anonymous Middle English lyrics
Performed 4 March 1988, Kleinhans Music Hall, Buffalo, New
      York; Thomas Swan, conductor, Buffalo Philharmonic
      Orchestra, Buffalo Schola Cantorum

The first thing that pops into my mind when I think about this piece is a funny incident during its composition. My studio is on the second floor of our house, with windows overlooking a park. I was working at the piano on a very hot summer day, wearing only Bermuda shorts, undershirt, no shoes, sweating profusely and singing very loudly some Latin phrase and banging out, over and over, a markedly dissonant chord. (Henry Cowell used to tell a story of the time he came upon Charles Ives doing exactly the same thing. He watched, fascinated, for several minutes and then asked in exasperation, "What in hell's name are you doing to that chord, Charley?" Ives replied, "I'm giving it the test of time.") Suddenly, that odd feeling that someone was watching struck me. I looked toward the open window, which now framed a man's shoulders and face, staring at me with an amazed expression that mixed bewilderment and fright. The window is at least sixteen feet above the ground, so the look on my face must have mirrored his. Then I remembered: this was the day the window sashes were to be painted. The man quickly vanished and soon I heard him telling a coworker in a stage whisper, "Watch your step: a crazy guy lives upstairs."

Te Deum is my only choral work with a symphony orchestra accompaniment, and it is one of those pieces that seemed to turn out better than I hoped or expected. When I first played through the score for the conductor and his colleagues, it was obvious they experienced the same happy surprise I did, but the best confirmation came from Carolyn. She had not heard a note of the work until the final rehearsal of chorus and orchestra in the dark auditorium at Buffalo. Usually she sits alone at rehearsals and I wander about. She remained in her seat when the rehearsal ended, and as I approached I saw on her face a look of incredulity. I had never before seen her overwhelmed by a work of mine.

As I've done previously in religious pieces, the circle of fifths is used, that is, starting on a tone and proceeding up or down by fifths until it passes through all other eleven tones and ends up at its beginning again. It strikes me as the perfect musical metaphor for God, and it appears in numerous guises throughout the entire work. I was particularly pleased with the way it worked out in the *Patrem immensae majestatis* movement, which is harmonized exclusively with chords built on a repeating progression of ascending fifths. Like several earlier choral works (notably *Jonah and the Whale*), *Te Deum* also employs a macaronic text, equally divided between liturgical Latin and Middle English poetry, and that arrangement accounts for the piece's subtitle, which translates to "the word of God with the word of the people."

The Vatican has received mixed reviews over its decision in the early 1960s to allow the Mass to be celebrated either in the customary Latin or in the congregation's native tongue. Many have decried the loss of the sense of ritual and tradition that Latin provided and are unhappy with the mundanity of a modern-language substitute. Others have welcomed the change because communicants can finally understand everything the priest is saying. The idea for this work was to reconcile both points of view: to maintain the ritualistic patina that colors Saint Augustine's beautiful prayer and to intersperse its various sections with fourteenth-century poems that more or less paraphrase in English the faith and praise expressed in Latin. The opening phrases here may illustrate the principle (and also why I preferred to incorporate the old English poetry instead of relying on the standard translation):

Te Deum laudamus;
    te Dominum confitemur.
(We praise thee, O God;
    we acknowledge thee to be the Lord.)
Te æternum Patrem
    omnis terra veneratur.
(All the earth doth worship thee,
    the Father everlasting.)

Light! Light! thou Faderes brightnesses,
    Thou trust and hope of alle,
List what thy folk throughout the world
    To thee biddeth and calle.
Him hevene and erthe and wilde see
    And all that is ther-on
Wroughte, of thy cominge
    [Praise him] with blisfol [song.]

The Aspern Papers
(1987)

∾

Opera in two acts
116 minutes
Libretto by the composer, based on the novella by Henry James
Performed 19 November 1988, Music Hall, Dallas, Texas;
    Frederica von Stade, mezzo; Elizabeth Söderström, soprano;
    Richard Stilwell, baritone; Neil Rosenshein, tenor; Eric
    Halfvarson, bass; Katherine Ciesinski, mezzo; Nicola
    Rescigno, conductor; Mark Lamos, director

The Minnesota Orchestra's final stop on its national tour with Neville conducting and Flicka singing *Casa Guidi* was the Kennedy Center in Washington. Neville and his wife, Flicka and her husband, and Carolyn and I had farewell drinks together at the Watergate. The tour had gone very well: Neville declared it the most satisfying commissioned work he had ever done, and Flicka simply adored doing the piece and it showed—I had never had a more loving performance of my music.

Before the party broke up I announced that I hoped to compose an opera for Flicka. So, several months later when Houston Grand Opera called about commissioning a work, I told them of my ambition. The intendant said he was not a von Stade fan, and that ended that as far as I was concerned. A commission from the Washington

Opera came; they were interested in a new opera for her, but with one complication: because the Opera Theater was being renovated, it would need to be performed in the Kennedy Center's smaller Terrace Theater, which meant multiple performances stretched out over a month. When told of that arrangement, Flicka agreed to do it anyway. Her agent called (unbeknownst to her), asking me to reconsider the situation: she had acquiesced out of friendship, but the prolonged absence from her daughters would be a hardship for her. I understood perfectly and we canceled the project. Next, the Dallas Opera called: they had heard of my desire to write an opera for Flicka, and they already had her contracted for the 1988 season in Massenet's *Cendrillon* but would gladly replace that with whatever I wished to write for her.

By this time I had narrowed down the search for an appropriate subject to James's *The Aspern Papers.* The role of Tina was ideal for Flicka, and there were important parts for soprano, tenor, and baritone as well. I asked Flicka to mention some colleagues with whom she enjoyed working. Without hesitation she named Elizabeth Söderström (who had played the Marschallin to Flicka's Octavian in a *Rosenkavalier* I had seen) and Richard Stilwell (she had been Mélisande to his Pelléas). She had a phone number where I could reach Elizabeth during a current Met production. Being unknown to the famous diva, I was reluctant to phone, but when I did she could not have been more charming and happily accepted the role, as did Richard. With the addition of Neil Rosenshein in the title role, I could not have asked for a finer group of singer-actors, my own *Puritani* quartet. It was a dream cast and as a result we had a remarkably smooth, virtually flawless production, as a video of the telecast in PBS's *Great Performances* series clearly shows. I thought I'd never see another production to equal it, but I was wrong: a year or two later, *Aspern* was presented by the Royal Opera in Stockholm with Söderström repeating her role. What made it as memorable as the Dallas production was the more interesting set design and superb stage direction.

During rehearsals for the premiere, a reporter asked me if it was true Houston Grand Opera had turned down a chance to have the work written for them instead of Dallas. I said yes and explained why. We had an off-the-record agreement, but he went ahead and printed what I told him. On the morning the story appeared, everyone was disturbed that Flicka would be greatly upset when she saw the story. They urged me to tell her about it before she saw it in the newspapers. Carolyn and I took Flicka to lunch, and I tried to break the news to her as gently as possible. When I told her that a reporter, despite the off-the-record agreement, had printed what Houston's intendant said—that he was not a fan of hers—she simply laughed and replied, "Oh well, it doesn't matter. I knew that. They haven't asked me to go back there these past seven years."

Easter Day
(1988)

∾

Anthem for unaccompanied chorus
3 minutes
Poetry by Richard Crashaw
Performed 26 March 1988, Plymouth Congregational Church,
    Minneapolis, Minnesota; Philip Brunelle, conductor,
    Plymouth Congregational Church Choir

It is odd that choral music should form such a substantial portion of this catalogue given that my sole experience in choir singing was a sham. In
Rochester, Allen McHose, head of theory at Eastman and one of my
advisers, was also organist and conductor of the Brick Presbyterian
Church choir. Shortly after we arrived at Eastman, Carolyn auditioned for and was given the position of soprano soloist in his choir.
I decided to try out for the choir as well, primarily so that Carolyn
would not have to go to rehearsals alone but also because all the
choir members were fellow students. The basses were predominantly
composition majors, including our dear friend James Sutcliffe, and
they obligingly covered up all the gaffes I never failed to make. Even
today, my attempting to match a given tone will send Carolyn into
gales of laughter.

I don't remember much about the composing of *Easter Day* except that it was a request by Philip and a gift from me, intended to be paired with *Prelude for Easter Dawning*. Of the handful of short a cappella pieces I have written for the church, this one is a favorite, although I'm pretty sure it will never be popular because of its mild difficulty—a common complaint about my choral writing, I'm afraid. Part of the blame for the difficulty my music presents to church choirs can be attributed to my distaste for ninety percent of the choral music most frequently heard in churches and my determination not to write anything remotely resembling it. There is a thriving cottage industry of composers specializing in insipid, easy-to-take pieces for the "average" church choir. My objection has less to do with the simplism of these puerile concoctions than the complete absence of art, of anything vaguely challenging, and, most important, the wasting of opportunities to provide a worthwhile aesthetic experience for the congregation. Brunelle told me he had assumed that *Easter Day* would be the typical jubilant composition: fortissimo hosannahs and hallelujahs from the chorus matching the stridency of trumpets and drums. On the contrary, my anthem barely rises above a whisper and is unaccompanied: I pointed out that one of the lines in Crashaw's poem was "Of all the Gloryes Make Noone gay." It would not surprise me to learn, however, that the same poem has been set by someone in precisely the manner Philip anticipated.

The current state of church music is a melancholy reminder of what had once been among music's noblest achievements. The vast majority of today's compositions are not so much choral music as chordal music, that is, a progression of chords, often in parallel motion, while one of the greatest features of musical art—counterpoint—is all but unknown. Another dismal aspect of these pieces is accentuation and text setting. In the minds (and ears) of these purveyors of easy anthems, there is evidently no word in the English language that cannot be set to music using only eighth notes or quarter notes with perhaps an occasional triplet thrown in. I suspect that this nonchalant attitude regarding word setting was inspired by the early authors and composers of Protestant hymns who took a laissez-faire attitude toward prosody wherein (like the computer's ability to express everything under the sun using nothing but 0 and 1) any text can be set to music using nothing but quarter notes and half notes.

I once asked Carolyn's father, a Methodist minister and an enthusiastic hymn leader, the significance of those ubiquitous numbers—for example, 887. 887—printed beneath the titles of hymns. He explained that they represented the number of notes in each musical phrase of the hymn and are useful when adding a new or replacement stanza to that hymn (not an uncommon practice). So, for instance, in this case the first and second lines would need to be eight syllables long and the third line seven. Unbelievably, it seems immaterial whether these eight or seven syllables are in metrical feet of iambs, trochees, spondees, or anapests just so long as the number of syllables matches the number of notes! Consequently, the same tune sung to the words "Sion, praise thy Saviour, singing Hymns with exultation ringing, Praise thy King and Shepard true" is equally suitable for "With Hymns we praise the God above To bless us all with grace and love and teach us not to falter," although the accentuation comes out as "*With* Hymns *we* praise *the* God *above To* bless *us* all *with* grace *and* love *and* teach *us* not *to* falter."

Admittedly an extreme example, but illustrative of the prosodic callousness committed by many of those specializing in church music.

The Angel Israfil
(1989)

∞

Duet for two harps
6 minutes

The first thing to say about this piece is that the title is misspelled: the second *i* should be an *e*. I have no excuse for this aberration. Israfel (correctly spelled) is a character in *The Masque of Angels* and the title of one of the songs in *In Praise of Music*. After I returned the proofs of this piece to the publisher, the editor phoned me to point out the solecism, justifying a correction by saying they had just published a song titled "Israfel" by Leonard Bernstein. Apparently Poe's "Imp of the Perverse" was with me that day, for I was adamant that I was right and Bernstein was wrong. I felt so strongly that I didn't even bother to look it up, and I insisted that the editor leave it my way—after all, I had used it twice before in publications, so I should know. After the score appeared in print it finally occurred to me that I ought to check the spelling (just to be sure), and, regretfully, I now have to live with my arrogant error, although it isn't very likely that many people will ever be exposed to it.

The Angel Israfil first came into existence as a piano piece for four hands commissioned by an amateur pianist (a fellow professor at the university) fond of performing such pieces with his playing partner. I never heard the piece played publicly, and although the commissioner sent me a taped performance I did not enjoy it at all; I felt the conceit behind the piece misfired and I did not pursue publication. Poe's well-known poem, on which the piece is based, speaks metaphorically of Israfel's heartstrings as a "lute . . . By which he sits and sings / The trembling living wires / Of those unusual strings." Somehow the numerous twenty-note arpeggiated chords (meant to evoke the poem's central image) came off as a bit too modern and too cold on the piano, as well as not sounding appropriately angelic. For almost two decades the manuscript resided in the limbo of aborted sketches and unfinished works until I received a commission that immediately brought it back to mind. A gentleman whose wife and daughter were professional harpists wanted a surprise present to give his wife on her sixtieth birthday: a duet for two harps. With a little revision, the reborn version proved far more apt than the original. It has been published, although I can't imagine there is a very large market for harp duets.

Transforming this piece from its original instrumentation into a harp duet was, in effect, the death knell for half of the music I had written for solo piano and left the *Divertimento for Piano and Strings* in sole possession of the field. It is certainly curious that having begun my musical life with the ambition of becoming a pianist-composer, à la Chopin and Rachmaninoff, I am arriving at its end with but a single piece for solo piano in this catalogue—and that a very early work. I don't know how to account for this fact. Perhaps it is a form of revenge I have taken on the instrument because I was forced to renounce my dream of becoming a concertizing pianist. Yet composition has more than adequately compensated me for any loss and has been more rewarding artistically, I believe, than a performance career might have been. I am sure my subconscious must lean more toward gratitude than resentment for the change to a composition major.

During my junior year at Peabody I composed a *Piano Sonata* that I performed in the required senior recital the following year—my first and last public appearance as a solo pianist. Performing before an audience of my peers (my betters for the most part) did not turn out to be as exhilarating as I had once expected it would be. For a few seconds before attacking the piece—a few seconds that seemed to border on eternity—I was paralyzed with stage fright, my ice-cold hands suspended six inches above the keyboard. I was unable to re-member the opening notes of my own music. Abandoning all hope and foreseeing shame and ignominy, I simply allowed my hands to fall helplessly onto the keys. To my astonishment, the fingers struck the correct notes and the music started as if of its own accord, while I—dazed and amazed—became an onlooker, watching a stranger's hands move up and down the keyboard as if on automatic pilot. All in all, a frightening experience and I offered up a prayer of thanks that I had long ago forsaken the thought of making a progression of such experiences my profession.

Looking at the *Piano Sonata* the other day—for the first time in almost fifty years—reminded me of Nicholas Nabokov's good opin-ion of it. (It was unashamedly modeled after his own *Piano Sonata.*) I remember his amusement as he pointed out that the main theme of my slow movement was one note shy of being a twelve-tone row. I blushed, deeply embarrassed: Schoenberg was anathema in those days. I stammered, trying to explain that it had been unintention-al . . . I hadn't realized . . . I wasn't . . . A sharp burst of laughter interrupted my apologies; he slapped me on the knee and said, "It's all right. It's all right. I won't tell Igor Fyodorovich."

A Toccata of Galuppi's
(1989)

∾

Rhapsody for chamber choir, harpsichord, and string quartet
20 minutes
Poetry by Robert Browning
Performed 24 June 1990, Santa Fe, New Mexico; Larry Bandfield,
   conductor, Santa Fe Desert Chorale

The score of *Casa Guidi* begins with a simple musical phrase played on the piano. The text of the song that follows comes from a letter Elizabeth Browning wrote to her sister: "Robert wants a ducal bed for my room—all gilded and carving. I persuaded him to get a piano instead." Browning must have been an adequate if modest pianist to judge by the music he owned. He had obtained a book of Baldassare Galuppi toccatas at a flea market near the steps of the Florentine church of San Lorenzo, the same emporium where he bought a secondhand document relating a famous murder and trial in Rome that he eventually transformed into the long poem *The Ring and the Book*. No doubt something about those hundred-year-old keyboard compositions of Galuppi's elicited thoughts of mortality in the poet's mind, prompting him to ruminate on the decline of the grandeur of eighteenth-century Venice and his own frailty.

"A Toccata of Galuppi's" had always been one of my favorite poems by Browning, and I thought I saw a way of making an unusual choral work out of it: to have a string quartet accompany the chorus and an offstage or unseen harpsichord (not clavichord, as Browning has it—the volume would be too soft for my purposes) play Galuppi's music. Except for a few measures at the end, Galuppi's music would be quoted exactly as he wrote it, without anything altered or added, while the music of the string quartet and chorus would be a twelve-tone theme and variations. The intention was to audibly contrast the present time and a period long since vanished. To bolster that effect, the harpsichord would not be visible in the performance, only a spectral, sonic presence. The impression I wished to create in the listener's mind was that of the poet seated at a keyboard and envisioning an eighteenth-century Venetian world called into being as he actually plays the Galuppi toccata. I no longer remember what led me to think that Toccata no. 11 in B-flat was the one Browning had in mind: scholars continue to quarrel about it. Rightly or wrongly, it fit my idea and is the one I chose to use.

The two Italian cities that Carolyn and I have enjoyed more than any of the others are Florence and Venice—predilections, it seems, also shared by Robert Browning. He and his wife lived in Casa Guidi for fifteen years. Elizabeth died there and was buried in Florence's Protestant Cemetery. Eventually Robert moved on to Venice, residing in Cà Rezzonico with his son, Pen, until his death, at which time he was returned to London for interment in the Poets' Corner of Westminster Abbey. (His wish to be buried next to Elizabeth in Florence met with various difficulties and was denied.)

Our new Florence address was Borgo San Jacopo 13, a few steps west of the Ponte Vecchio and a block and a half from Casa Guidi. We have probably visited Robert's Venetian home as often as we have visited Casa Guidi, although in the case of Cà Rezzonico it was not only because it had served as a Browning residence; it also contains a representative collection of paintings by Longhi, Tiepolo, and Guardi and provides a fine example of eighteenth-century architecture and furnishings. (The dining room chairs in our Minneapolis home are copies made in Florence of the chairs in Cà Rezzonico.) Both of these dwellings stimulated musical ideas that are inextricably linked in my mind: *Casa Guidi,* discussed earlier in this catalogue, and *Galuppi,* which dawned on me as a possibility while standing on Cà Rezzonico's balcony overlooking the Grand Canal, musing on that enchanting, morose city. Turning back and peering into the deserted ballroom—vast and dark—the final lines of "A Toccata of Galuppi's" echoed in my head:

> "Dust and ashes!" So you creak it, and I want the heart to scold.
> Dear dead women, with such hair, too—what's become of all the gold
> Used to hang and brush their bosoms? I feel chilly and grown old.

Remarkably, the saturnine scenes of Venice that I looked upon from Cà Rezzonico's balcony were not Browning's inspiration for these lines: he composed the poem while he was still living at Casa Guidi in Florence.

Everyone Sang
(1991)

∾

Unaccompanied double chorus
5 minutes
Poetry by Siegfried Sassoon
Performed 20 April 1991, Heinz Hall, Pittsburgh, Pennsylvania;
1991 Pennsylvania All-State High School Chorus

One of the great poems to come out of World War I, "Everyone Sang" was first brought to my attention by Bernice Dalrymple, one of Minneapolis's grand dowagers and a committed arts patron. She lived a block from us on Mount Curve, and during the last decade of her life we were invited to her home every few days for cocktails or dinner. At Bernice's request, Carolyn and I gave a private recital in her home for a large party she hosted. At the end of the evening Carolyn was presented with a volume of modern poetry that Bernice, paraphrasing that wonderful line of Sassoon's, had inscribed: "For Carolyn, whose singing (for me) will never be done."

When I received a commission for a piece to be premiered at an All-State Chorus Conference in Pennsylvania, I chose Sassoon's poem in the hopes that high school students would find its upbeat mood appealing. Although they never complained (I could not attend the premiere in Pittsburgh), I recognize from their recording that they must have found it quite difficult. Not counting *Colonel Jonathan the Saint,* which deals with a situation in the aftermath of the Civil War, this is the only text directly related to war that I have ever set to music. That is probably due to a fluke of chronology: I was drafted into the army in 1945, immediately upon graduation from high school, and my service coincided with that brief peaceful hiatus between the conclusion of World War II and the outbreak of the Korean War. Consequently, my memories of the martial life are more benign than bellicose. During basic training, inductees took a test to discover whether they had an aptitude for Morse code. As the test proceeded, the dots and dashes, which had begun slowly, gradually got faster and faster. One by one the GIs around me dropped their pencils until I was the only one left scribbling. The examination was intended to test our speed and skill in distinguishing dots (short) and dashes (long), the raw material of telegraphy, but to me it was essentially a musical exercise in simple rhythmic dictation. As a result, the army felt I had an aptitude for cryptography and trained me as an intercept operator.

The overseas segment of my duty was served in Asmara, Eritrea—formerly an Italian colony—eavesdropping on the Soviet Air Force. A good many Italians still lived there, among them a maestro with a beautiful, snow-white mane and a young mistress, with whom he shared a tiny studio apartment. I arranged to take lessons in exchange for a variety of PX items such as candy, soap, and cigarettes. Up to this time, I had had only two years of piano lessons plus some autodidactic gleanings in harmony and orchestration, courtesy of York's public library. I have no real memory of what actually transpired in those lessons (the mistress always excused herself and disappeared into a closet-sized kitchenette). I do remember analyzing some short classical piano pieces but nothing else in the way of theoretical studies.

My work in piano came to naught since I had neither time nor opportunity to practice. My final lesson in the Italian's one-room flat is the clearest recollection I have of those meetings: he presented me with a large score—more than a hundred manuscript pages of beautiful calligraphy—a long composition titled *Il ritorno di gloria,* clearly no longer destined to celebrate a fascist victory, saying that perhaps the United States now had a use for it. The music, I immediately recognized, was mostly plagiarized from the concluding movement of Respighi's *Pines of Rome.* I took the score back to my base, but because it was large and bulky, I left it in Africa when I returned to the States.

Thinking about it today, almost sixty years later, the abandonment of his heroic opus can still summon up a blush, even though I know the music was worthless, for vanquished or victor. On the other hand, the maestro provided one vivid musical memory that can change that blush into a smile: with a ragtag orchestra of nine players and five singers, he rescored, staged, sang, and conducted the first and funniest production I ever saw of *Rigoletto.*

The Dream of Valentino
(1993)

Opera in two acts
135 minutes
Libretto by Charles Nolte
Performed 15 January 1994, Kennedy Center, Washington, D.C.;
    Robert Brubaker, tenor; Suzanne Murphy, soprano; Julian
    Patrick, bass; Dan Dressen, tenor; Christopher Keene,
    conductor, Washington Opera

The Florence apartment we rented
several times in the early nineties was
at Por Santa Maria 5, half a block north of the Ponte Vecchio, completing the encirclement of that bridge, as our previous apartments
had been located to its east, south, and west as well as at its foot. Like
two of our previous Florentine dwellings, this apartment was on the
seventh floor and boasted two terraces. A small studio up a spiral
stairway featured a window overlooking acres and acres of red tiled
rooftops. Much of *The Dream of Valentino* was composed there.

I have often used this catalogue to write of a blunder or
miscalculation—something that did not go quite as one might have
wished—in the composition or premiere of a work. *Valentino* provides
the most egregious instance. Soon after I had completed the first act,
the Dallas Opera phoned me with what they considered to be good

news: Marcello Giordano, at the time a fast-rising tenor, had agreed to create the leading role. He was perfect, they felt: handsome, his English only slightly accented, wonderful voice, and so on. There was only one problem: he had seen a copy of act I and liked it, but he said it would suit him much better if his part were just a little higher, "to let the sunshine in, you know?" Glad to comply, I transposed his part in act I up a whole step, made all the necessary and numerous adjustments, and started composing act 2 with sunshine foremost in mind. By the time the score was finished and duplicated, Signor Giordano withdrew from the production. I never learned why he was unable to fulfill his contract, probably a more lucrative engagement with the Metropolitan. The tenor who ultimately created the role for the Washington premiere (as well as another tenor who performed the part the following year in Dallas) justly complained of the high tessitura. But by then the score had been published, and it was too late to do anything about it.

That blunder was compounded by an additional misstep. Shortly before I received the commission to write *Valentino, The Aspern Papers* had been performed in Stockholm at the Royal Opera. It had been wonderfully staged by a Swedish director, Ann-Margaret Pettersson. At a postperformance supper party I told her how much I admired her work and promised that I would try to get her to stage my next opera. When *Valentino* was finished I told the Washington Opera that I would like Ann-Margaret to direct. They negotiated and agreed to her two conditions: that she be paid a thousand dollars more than their usual fee and, knowing that Dallas was coproducing, that she also be hired to direct the opera there. Despite her great directorial ability, it turned out that she had very little feeling for Hollywood, the 1920s, or the Jazz Age. As a result of my offhand promise, the Washington premiere failed to create the aura that was wanted. Worse, since her terms had been accepted, we were not allowed to substitute a different director for the subsequent production in Dallas, and despite numerous suggestions—from librettist, composer, and one of the singers—for improving the staging (and decor as well), the much-needed Hollywood atmosphere was still lacking.

I have no wish to exculpate my own participation in whatever shortcomings or faults *Valentino* may have: my selection of the Hollywood legend as an operatic subject may well have been the first mistake. There is an inherent problem with operas about modern-day individuals. Operas dealing with Valentino, Nixon, Harvey Milk, Malcolm X, Marilyn Monroe, and Charles Lindbergh have not been as well received as those about Poe, Boris Godunov, Lizzie Borden, Simon Boccanegra, Baby Doe, or Wozzeck. The reason, I maintain, is that a certain removal in time, a historical distance from the opera's audience, or some degree of exceptional behavior is required before a real person is fully believable as a singing character. Persons like Monroe and Nixon are so well known to audiences that it is hard to accept their breaking into song. But once the patina of history or myth envelopes them—as in the case, say, of Lizzie Borden or Poe—the suspension of belief is greatly facilitated. In the case of *Valentino,* I had concluded that with the passage of three-quarters of a century, he had graduated from newsreels and magazines into the realm of legend and romance. It may well be that my assessment was a bit premature.

There was a lavish postpremiere supper at the Kennedy Center, attended by the designer Valentino and his large entourage from Italy (all gorgeously accoutred), along with many prominent citizens as well as government and diplomatic figures. At our table of ten, Carolyn was partnered with the Italian ambassador, Boris Bianchieri, directly across from where I was seated next to his wife. She asked me what my next project was going to be. I told her that I yearned to make an opera of Giuseppe Lampedusa's great novel *The Leopard,* but it had proved impossible to obtain the rights from the Lampedusa Estate. She gave a little laugh and called across the table to her husband, "Boris, can you imagine what this gentleman wants his next opera to be? *Il gattopardo.*" She turned to me and said, "Lampedusa's widow is Boris's aunt." Before the evening ended, the ambassador promised he would speak to his aunt on my behalf when he returned to Italy for summer vacation and would contact me in the fall when he came back to Washington. I heard nothing from him that fall. I wrote reminding him of his promise, but never received an answer.

To God
"In memoriam M. B. 1994"
(1994)

∾

Anthem for chorus and offstage trumpet
3 minutes
Poetry by Richard Crashaw
Performed 25 September 1994, Plymouth Congregational
    Church, Minneapolis, Minnesota; Philip Brunelle,
    conductor, Plymouth Congregational Church Choir

Still another request from Brunelle, and one I happily honored since I, too, wished to pay tribute to the M. B. of the title. For twenty-four years Marlene Baver was the deputy organist and choirmaster at Plymouth Congregational Church. Philip wrote of her: "She was a musical factotum whose talents included the obvious conducting and playing, being 'ears' for balance and 'fetcher' for missing music; she was also a woman whose musical talents included flute and trumpet, in addition to the keyboard and percussion instruments. On any composition that had three trumpet parts, Marlene always played third." That inventory of her many abilities accurately portrays a woman whose life was devoted to music but omits an important facet of her personality: a ready and unusually hearty sense of humor.

I cannot remember ever having a conversation with her, however brief, that did not provoke laughter from both parties.

The score of *To God* alludes to Marlene in several ways. In the text where Crashaw speaks of "John, (Who writ that heavenly Revelation)," the chorus quotes a couple of measures from my oratorio *The Revelation of Saint John the Divine,* which Marlene had once helped prepare for performance. The other allusion is obvious: when the chorus arrives at the last word of the text and holds the final chord for almost one minute, a solo unseen trumpet is heard playing a simple melody whose notes never rise above the staff. A suitable solo for third trumpeter alone. At first I was a bit concerned that anyone unaware of the raison d'être for this unexpected coda wagging the body of the piece might find the ending cryptic or capricious. I was pleased to discover that that did not turn out to be the case. A number of listeners have said they found it reassuring or comforting, even transcendent, to hear the trumpet's serene postlude floating out above the sustained voices. Although I'm getting credit for something I hadn't really contemplated, I am loath to dismiss it. Perhaps I realized the effect it would create. To paraphrase Cocteau: the artist never does anything unconsciously; he just doesn't know he did it.

One could assume that the preponderance of religious choral works in this catalogue is a reflection of its author's own inclinations, but I must confess that I cannot tell whether that is true. Organized religions, as such, hold no appeal for me even though I was sent to a parochial grade school. It would be false to say I was raised a Catholic, since there was very little religious practice in my home life as I was growing up. My parents raised no objections when I told them I did not want to continue on into Catholic junior and senior high school: I was put off by the self-righteousness and smugness of the nuns who taught at Saint Patrick's, and I suffered several instances of outright cruelty at their hands. The punishment for failing to respond word for word with the correct answer to a catechism question—we were forced to learn the answers by rote and consequently they seemed meaningless to us—was particularly harsh. From time to time, after adolescence, I attended Protestant churches of various denominations—primarily churches where Carolyn had been engaged as the soprano soloist. Although I usually enjoyed the music much more, I felt in every other way that they compared palely with the costumes, incense, ceremony, and ritual of their competitor. I never understood why preachers felt they had to spend twenty minutes every Sunday explicating a few lines of an ancient text that were perfectly clear to anyone with an average IQ.

Today it is difficult to find one area of conflict on the globe not fueled by one organized religion in opposition to another. Given the power, I would gladly split up religions into millions of private, invisible churches, each consisting of a congregation of one. The music might not be as inspiring, and for some the postservice socializing would be a distinct loss, but I think the peace and harmony of the world could be greatly improved.

Valentino Dances
(1994)

∾

Suite of tangos from the opera *The Dream of Valentino*
12 minutes
Performed 13 July 1994, Orchestra Hall, Minneapolis, Minnesota;
David Zinman, conductor, Minnesota Orchestra

Years before David Zinman premiered *Valentino Dances* with the Minnesota Orchestra at a Sommerfest concert, he had commissioned a work for the Baltimore Symphony, for which he was principal conductor. The resulting composition was *Le Tombeau d'Edgar Poe*. In our first discussion about a work for Baltimore, when I asked what sort of piece he had in mind, I was surprised to hear him say, "I can imagine a great twelve-to fifteen-minute tango from you; you know, a kind of tango version of Ravel's *La valse*." Nothing at that time could have seemed more foreign to me, and I quickly dismissed the suggestion. Later, when the idea of writing an opera about Rudolph Valentino began to form in my mind, I realized that the tango would have to be one of the more important elements in telling his story in music. By the time the opera was finished I discovered what David had intuited long before: I could write a pretty good tango and have great fun doing it. Consequently, when there came a request for something David could do at Sommerfest, I reverted to his original proposal for the Baltimore piece.

The opera contains three tangos, each associated with a different stage of Valentino's career: the first as a newly arrived immigrant working as a taxi dancer in New York; the second at a Hollywood party given by Alla Nazimova during which he proposes to and is accepted by Natasha; the third after an injunction bans his participation in films and he is forced to perform in vaudeville houses to earn his living. In *Valentino Dances* (and the word *dances* is intended here as a verb, not a plural noun), all three tangos are presented in that chronological order, but other material is introduced as well and everything is reorchestrated for an instrumentation approximately twice the size called for in the opera. The suite also includes what amounts to a *concertante* role for an instrument I had never used before: the piano accordion. It was not actually used in the opera itself but parroted instead by a synthesizer.

I hadn't purposely been avoiding the accordion (there isn't much use for it in serious music anyway), but I will admit to a longstanding distaste for it. Around 1940, a new music store—Lopez's Music House—opened in York. Door-to-door salesmen combed the neighborhoods, encouraging parents to purchase instruments and music lessons for their progeny. My father liked the idea and decided that I, going on fourteen, should learn to play an instrument. What would I like? For no known reason, I said, "Drums." I was told to try again. "Trumpet?" Too loud. My father decided I liked the accordion. Soon I was lugging that heavy instrument in its awkward-shaped case the eight blocks from home to Lopez's Music House, enduring an excruciating thirty-minute lesson, then lugging it back. I learned to read music and to play a few simple tunes (using the left hand only to push and pull the bellows, not to press the buttons), but I despised the instrument and was embarrassed by its immigrant status.

Within a year the lessons were mercifully ended, but an awakened interest in music burgeoned. In my father's café on Saturday nights, there was live music for dancing. On Sundays, the café was closed and I began to use the old upright piano there to teach myself to play with both hands. I loved the piano but could only use it on Sundays. As my sixteenth birthday was approaching, my parents asked what gift I would like to mark the occasion. Since there was no longer dancing at the café—World War II was now at full tilt—the old upright was no longer needed there. Could it be moved to our home where I might use it every day and could I take piano lessons? Fine. On that sixteenth birthday, I raced home from school, eager to see if the transfer had already been made; I ran into the room where I hoped to find the upright piano. It was not there. But where it should have been, there stood—unbelievably—the most gorgeous, brand-new, black baby grand piano imaginable. No other gift has ever meant as much to me.

Spirituals and Swedish Chorales (1994)

∞

Cycle for unaccompanied chorus
12 minutes
Original spirituals by John Olon-Scrymgeour; Swedish chorales,
    sixteenth and eighteenth centuries
Performed 25 September 1994, Ted Mann Auditorium,
    University of Minnesota, Minneapolis, Minnesota; Philip
    Brunelle, conductor, Plymouth Music Series Chorus

This work was a gift commemorating the thirtieth anniversary of the Plymouth Music Series, an organization that has championed my music, both choral and instrumental, for many years. I do not know why I enjoy assembling and setting macaronic texts, but I do. In some instances these texts are created simply by placing Latin and vernacular texts cheek by jowl, as was done in *Te Deum* and *Jonah.* Here, it was a matter of juxtaposing two different modern languages.

What most intrigued me about placing these severe and solemn Swedish chorales of the sixteenth and eighteenth centuries alongside the more freewheeling and exuberant African American spirituals of a much later period is the sharp difference in their modes of expressing profound religious fervor and the striking contrast of the musical manner in these two types of devotional music, even though the verbal matter or message is remarkably similar. I was also interested in contrasting the musical expression of the stern, frigid North versus the relaxed, warm South. That idea comes from Monteverdi's theory of *i contrasti,* where he uses the image of an ailing infant revived by alternating hot and cold baths as justification for the alternation of serious and comic scenes in his opera *L'incoronazione di Poppea.* Fortunately I did not need to know even a bit of Swedish language or pronunciation to write this piece; the chorale tunes and texts are authentic examples from historical hymnals. My sole contribution was to harmonize the tunes in a mildly dissonant fashion to emphasize a quality of harshness I wished them to convey.

The words and music of the spirituals, on the other hand, are not at all authentic but only my attempts to emulate the style. I wrote them thirty-five years earlier to serve as local color in my post—Civil War opera, *Colonel Jonathan the Saint.* Despite the failure of that first full-length opera, I have always had a soft spot for its offstage spirituals. At the opera's premiere in Denver, a large choir from a local black church was hired to sing them, which more than compensated for their want of authenticity. (Apparently some people have been fooled: I've seen several programs where following the titles is "as arranged by D. Argento.") In addition to the fine rendition the choir gave at the premiere, they honored me by singing my spirituals in their own Sunday morning church services.

No one has had as great an influence on my career as Philip Brunelle, one of my oldest acquaintances in Minneapolis. We first met when he was a student in my History of Opera course at the university. As performer, he was percussionist in the premiere of *The Revelation of Saint John* and pianist for the Minnesota Orchestra in the premiere of *Bravo Mozart!* He commissioned and led the premiere of *Jonah* and conducted the premiere of a number of operas: *Postcard from Morocco* (and its national tour), *The Voyage of Edgar Allan Poe* (in the United States and in Sweden), *Water Bird Talk* (at Brooklyn's Academy of Music), and *Miss Havisham's Wedding Night.* He recorded a CD of my choral music as well as *Jonah, Postcard, Variations for Orchestra,* and *Te Deum.* He organized a splendid three-concert retrospective of my music at the Walker Art Center and had multiple celebratory events arranged for my sixtieth birthday (and even got Garrison Keillor to host one of them). He was equally active in arranging similar celebrations of my seventieth and seventy-fifth birthdays.

Like a number of other choral works in this catalogue, *Spirituals and Swedish Chorales* was not a commission but a gift—a surprise this time—to Philip and the Plymouth Music Series (nowadays called VocalEssence). The music he performs in his position as organist-choirmaster in Minneapolis and the numerous conducting engagements he has had in Sweden are responsible for suggesting the piece's odd combination of musics. This and other works of mine can only partially repay the numerous gifts and support I have received from Philip and his organization. His longtime advocacy and friendship have been invaluable to me.

Miss Havisham's Fire (revised) (1995)

∽

Opera in two acts plus a prologue and epilogue
123 minutes
Libretto by John Olon-Scrymgeour, after *Great Expectations* by
    Charles Dickens; revised by the composer
Performed 3 June 2001, Loretto-Hilton Center, Saint Louis,
    Missouri; Erie Mills, soprano; Beatrice Jona Affron,
    conductor, Opera Theatre of Saint Louis

Sixteen years passed before I had sufficient objectivity to proceed with the
revision of this opera. Or perhaps I should say it took that long for
the disappointment to die down sufficiently so that I could face the
task with equanimity. From time to time during those years, I looked
at the score with the intention of revising it, but after a few minutes
enthusiasm dissipated and I returned the music to the shelf. I felt
the biggest problem with the piece was a result of attempting to fulfill
Beverly Sills's desire to have an encyclopedic vehicle that would leave
her "as wrung out as a rag" when she finished singing it. (Often, she
claimed, her voice was just achieving the shape she wanted when the
final curtain fell.)

The revision, once begun in earnest, was surprisingly clear and
easy, consisting as it did of deleting four or five scenes that I consid-

ered expendable (to reduce the two eighty-minute acts to less than sixty minutes each), rearranging the remaining scenes (to make the chronology clearer), cutting superfluous lines everywhere, and stringently shortening the closing mad scene. Before making these alterations, I sent the librettist a three-page letter detailing the revised synopsis, outlining the changes and deletions I proposed to make, and asking for his opinion, disagreement, or approval. He never replied. Five years later, after the revision's premiere had been announced, we spoke, and I politely rebuked him for his nonparticipation. He swore that he really had written a response to my proposal (in which he fully agreed with the revision) but that only recently—alas—he discovered the letter among his papers: he had forgotten to mail it! The hardest part of the revision was technical, not artistic: pages of the score and parts had been so shuffled about, crossed out, cut and pasted that no copyist could possibly decipher them. I computer-engraved all the material myself, a labor of love and well worth it. It was more than gratifying to earn the best reviews I ever had with a work that was once thoroughly rejected.

Despite extraordinarily enthusiastic audience response and laudatory reviews, it appears that this opera, too, has fallen into an all-too-familiar obscurity. Not entirely unexpected, considering that *Postcard, Poe, Aspern* and *Casanova* were also greeted with almost equal enthusiasm by press and public and have, for all intents and purposes, drifted into the category we gently term "neglected." There is no point bewailing the situation or becoming embittered. Any number of reasons might explain the evanescence of contemporary music. Prime among them, I suggest, is the fact that the repertorial depositories are not only brimful but overflowing. Most American opera companies are more than content to present an eternal rotation of the same two dozen eighteenth- and nineteenth-century classics. From time to time, to assuage some minor pangs of guilt, a contemporary work might make a showing, then it's quickly back to status quo. Even *Wozzeck*, now three-quarters of a century old, is still considered a risky undertaking. The symphonic repertory is no better: at least ninety percent of every season is made up of the perennial Mozart, Beethoven, Brahms, and their lesser but equally familiar contemporaries. The most recent score that can claim a foothold in orchestral literature is Bartók's *Concerto for Orchestra,* a work composed more than half a century ago. So it may well be that composers will have to accept that their works—like automobiles, fashions, celebrities—are good for only a couple of seasons at best, and equally disposable.

One might assume from this observation that audiences prefer gazing upon their gentler and kinder reflections in eighteenth- and nineteenth-century music to confronting the harsher realities recent music shows them. On the other hand, the problem may merely be one of supply and demand. There are certainly far more artists per capita today than ever before. I don't know how many composers were practicing in Vienna in 1790, but I'm sure that number, proportionally, is minuscule compared to the thousands and thousands now vying for attention in New York City alone. The American Composers Forum claims that my own modest area—Saint Paul and Minneapolis—harbors six hundred. As with the sorcerer's apprentice, the supply has hopelessly swamped the demand. A modest proposal: works like Beethoven's Ninth, Schubert's *Unfinished, Aïda,* and *Faust* could be given sabbaticals of, say, five years. They'd gain greatly by returning to our ears refreshed and at the same time clear a bit of space for performing organizations to explore new repertory.

Valse Triste
(1996)

∾

Sixtieth birthday greeting for David Zinman, for harp and strings
2 minutes
Performed 10 July 1996, Orchestra Hall, Minneapolis, Minnesota;
David Zinman, conductor, Minnesota Orchestra

Of the various trifles I have written over the years (birthday greetings, album leaves, wedding processionals), this is the only one I allowed to be published, primarily because it was included in a CD of my music released by the Minnesota Orchestra. It was premiered during a Sommerfest concert of the orchestra conducted by David Zinman on his sixtieth birthday. I and nineteen others—a virtual Who's Who of living American composers whose works David had premiered—had been asked to contribute a brief musical salute to him. Considering arrival at the age of sixty to be either a farewell to middle age or cause for celebration, I decided to emphasize the former and stress, in a playfully mock tone, the rueful rather than joyful aspect of the occasion. Stated simply: I wrote a sad version of "Happy Birthday to You." With its three-four meter sufficiently slowed down and with the minor cast I gave it, the first title that occurred to me was *Valse Triste.*

I must have done a better job of transforming the tune than I realized: one reviewer, who evidently doesn't read liner notes, spoke of being disturbed by the surprising resemblance, at just one or two spots, to "Happy Birthday." Another reviewer showed off his musicological acumen by pointing out that my title had been previously used by Sibelius, unaware that the title was not unique to him but generic. In my youth, most amateur pianists had anthologies of popular short and easy pieces (Sibelius's waltz was one) that rarely appeared on recital programs (except, perhaps, as encores) but were played solely for the pianist's own enjoyment or the enjoyment of others; typical items were Chaminade's *Scarf Dance,* Debussy's *Reverie,* Cui's *Orientale,* Paderewski's *Minuet in G,* Rubinstein's *Melody in F,* Rachmaninoff's *Prelude in C-sharp Minor,* and many others. I suppose that amateurs still buy these volumes and enjoy entering the world of music through them just as I did, but I can't think of any composer today who would dream of writing a piece so simple and pleasant, something that's fun to play. And that, I think, is truly regrettable.

During the two years I studied piano in York (from age sixteen until I was drafted into the army at age eighteen) progress was surprisingly rapid, even to the point—after I completed my military service—of being accepted into the Peabody Conservatory's piano program, where most of my fellow piano majors had a head start of at least six or more years. My piano teacher in York was a small, courtly, and charming gentleman with white hair and mustache—rather like the Little King or a miniature Pierre Monteux—known to everyone as Professor Link (I'm sure the title was self-bestowed). My lessons were on Mondays at 6 p.m., and he was usually still at the dinner table when I arrived. I spent a good part of the lesson time suppressing a smile or titter because, as I played my scales or some of the pieces cited above, they were often accompanied, not unpleasantly, by the gentle gurgling of his digestive system and poorly masked belches.

He seemed to have a genuine fondness for me because, unlike his other students, I loved to practice and was always well prepared. I was already composing little piano pieces, and in time I became emboldened enough to show them to him. I'm sure he didn't know what to make of them, but the fact that I had done my manuscript in ink instead of pencil impressed him. He used one of the standard piano methods of the day, something divided into twelve grades (I reached level 10) but often supplemented it with what I'd now regard as odd choices, although at the time I simply enjoyed them: a piano reduction of the slow movement of Beethoven's Fifth Symphony, a simplified version of the opening of Tchaikovsky's *B-flat minor Piano Concerto* (much the rage then). My last assignment from him was Beethoven's *Appassionata Sonata*—way over my head.

Many years later, when I was sure he'd forgotten his promising young piano student who failed to make it through the conservatory, my parents sent me his obituary in which he was quoted as claiming me as his proudest achievement, though I'm fairly certain he never heard a note of my music.

Walden Pond
(1996)

∾

Cycle for chorus, three celli, and harp
25 minutes
Excerpts from *Walden* by Henry David Thoreau
Performed 26 October 1996, Ted Mann Auditorium, University
    of Minnesota, Minneapolis, Minnesota; Dale Warland,
    conductor, Dale Warland Singers

F or some reason, bodies of water—rivers,
lakes, seas—hold a great fascination for
me. Among the various titles in this catalogue are *Jonah and the Whale, A
Water Bird Talk, To Be Sung upon the Water,* and *The Voyage of Edgar Allan Poe.* Even
where no hint of some aquatic orientation is in the title of a work,
the action is frequently located near or on a body of water: *The Aspern
Papers* occurs on the banks of Lake Como; *Casanova's Homecoming* is set
in Venice; *Colonel Jonathan the Saint* takes place on Maryland's Eastern
Shore; even *The Andrée Expedition* attempts to traverse the frozen Arctic.
Several other works that, at one time or other, I considered but never
actually undertook or left unfinished show the same absorption. For
example, one libretto I completed but never set to music was titled
The Berengaria Exchange, and its action transpired entirely aboard a luxury
ocean liner as it crossed the Atlantic during the week of the great Wall

Street crash. (*Valentino,* too, contains an extended scene aboard an ocean liner.) A composition in progress remains unfinished as this catalogue goes to press; complete information about it is lacking, but it ought to be mentioned that its title is *Four Seascapes for Chorus and Orchestra,* the various sections dealing with ocean (Melville's Pacific), sea (Thorton Wilder's Mediterranean), river (Twain's Mississippi), and lake (Henry James's Como).

Of all these compositions, *Walden Pond* would be the one work most unabashedly related to this preoccupation, using it not merely as a circumstance or colorful backdrop, but focusing directly on a body of water itself. And that may explain why I prefer *Walden* to all my other larger choral pieces, as do some of my friends. What pleases me most about the work is the idyll-like savor it has. Naturally much of it is due to Thoreau's beautiful text, which I edited freely and extensively in order to obtain the specific images I wanted. But a good part of the ambience of the piece is due to the instrumentation: the harp lends a properly watery, rippling tone while the three celli add a sense of warmth, darkness, and depth. (The use of multiple solo celli is borrowed from Rossini's *William Tell* overture, in which their sound wonderfully limns a placid woodland.)

Two of the last four entries dealt with my preconservatory days, so that topic might as well be continued here. About the time I was thirteen, I discovered the wonders of the Martin Memorial Library, a brand-new public facility near our home. Above each stack in the children's wing, signs identified the subjects, and because I was obsessed with building model airplanes, I was first drawn to the stack marked "Models." I read all there was about building models. A stack close by was labeled "Mystery," and, thanks to Nancy Drew and Carolyn Keene, I became and remain an inveterate reader of detective stories. (And it is still mysteries written by women like Ruth Rendell and P. D. James that I favor.)

Sometime between the age of fourteen and fifteen, I began paying attention to another stack flanked by those two. I had heard (and then bought) a recording of Gershwin's *Rhapsody in Blue*. There in the "Music" section was his biography. I read it. It mentioned Stravinsky, whom I had never heard of. I took out his autobiography (and bought a recording of *Le sacre du printemps*). Stravinsky spoke of Rimsky-Korsakov. I read his *Chronicles* (and bought a recording of *Sheherazade*). I continued back through the history of music (visiting the adults' wing to find some composers) until I reached Bach—as far back as I then cared to go. At the same time, a kindly librarian permitted me (I was underage) to use their record collection and listening room whereby I first became acquainted with a great deal of musical literature. Better yet, I also discovered that while biographies were housed in wings of the main floor, a veritable gold mine of technical books on music—theory, harmony counterpoint, orchestration, even music appreciation and aesthetics—existed down in the library's dim bowels. I was given access to them and thus began an intense period of autodidactic activity.

I tried to absorb everything on view and can still recall, after sixty years, my annoyance with the author of the instrumentation text who held up Johann Strauss's "Beautiful Blue Danube" as a paradigm of the orchestrator's skill. To a teenager who couldn't get enough of Stravinsky's *Le sacre* or *Petrushka,* Strauss's pretty waltz seemed a pallid choice for teaching a student how to score music. Books on matters unrelated to composition didn't interest me, although one of them has always stayed with me because of its intriguing title: *Music for the Man Who Enjoys "Hamlet."* I didn't remember very much about the book, but I more or less confiscated the title as my personal slogan.

Even before I had my first piano lesson, I was starting to compose little pieces. One of these was a first attempt at an orchestral piece, *Polka for Flute and Orchestra* (scarcely a minute long and baldly plagiarized from Shostakovich's *Polka* from his *Age of Gold* ballet). With the audacity of youth, I phoned the conductor of the York Symphony, Sylvan Levin (he conducted the Lancaster and Main Line Orchestras as well). When I asked for a meeting to show him my score, he hesitated, obviously gauging my age pretty accurately, but finally, we made an appointment for a few days later at 4 p.m. When I rang his bell, he opened the door and stepped out onto the porch, closing the door behind him. He was wearing coat, hat, and gloves. (I had fantasized that he would go to the piano, sight-read the full score perfectly—as I had read about in the composers' biographies—evince astonishment, and eagerly schedule the premiere for his next concert.) Instead, he said he was on his way to his eye doctor but could spare a minute or two. "Where's the score?" I gave it to him. He stood there and examined it for all of ten seconds, then handed it back. "How old are you?" I told him. "Just fifteen? Well, give yourself another fifteen years and you might come up with something worthwhile." Without another word, he headed for his ocular rendezvous, leaving me on the porch, devastated and near tears. Fifteen years! That was a lifetime, an eternity! Yet, despite the hurtfulness of that prognosis, his estimate turned out to be oracular: shortly before my thirtieth birthday I concluded my studies at the Eastman School, where I had composed a ballet, a concerto for soprano and orchestra, and a chamber opera, all three of which Howard Hanson would deem worthy of inclusion on his Festival of American Music—officially my coming-out party— alongside the likes of such compositional icons as Roger Sessions, Aaron Copland, and Roy Harris.

What got me interested in composition? Looking back, I'd say it was inevitable. My early interests and pursuits—building models, reading mysteries, working puzzles, repairing things, deciphering codes—all revolve around the same principle: problem solving. And, in my view, writing a poem, painting a picture, or composing a song is in large measure only a higher form of problem solving.

A Few Words about Chekhov
(1996)

∾

Seven songs for mezzo, baritone, and piano; orchestrated in 2001
20 minutes
Letters of Anton Chekhov and a memoir by Olga Knipper
Performed 12 October 1996, Ordway Theater, Saint Paul,
      Minnesota; Frederica von Stade, mezzo; Håkan Hagegård,
      baritone; Martin Katz, piano
Orchestral version performed 22 March 2003, Ordway Music
      Theater, Saint Paul, Minnesota; Kimberly Barber, mezzo;
      Håkan Hagegård, baritone; Andreas Delfs, conductor,
      Saint Paul Chamber Orchestra

A Few Words about Chekhov is part of a trilogy of cycles commissioned by the Schubert Club, the other two being *From the Diary of Virginia Woolf* and *The Andrée Expedition.* The first cycle was for mezzo, the second for baritone, and this one for mezzo and baritone. I seem to prefer mezzos to sopranos and baritones to tenors: the leading roles in most of my operas are for either or both of these voice types. Without intending it, I now notice that all three cycles share certain characteristics: they are person-oriented and exhibit a seriousness of purpose not present in their other siblings, and all three conclude with the protagonist's death. The greater weightiness of these cycles is a reflection of the commissioner they have in common and the specific audience that he has cultivated, perhaps the most discerning group of music lovers in this area. I have always been as concerned about the kind of listeners for whom I am writing as I have been about the performers themselves.

At the start of rehearsals for the premiere of this work (in the piano version), the baritone, Håkan Hagegård, felt strongly that he and Frederica von Stade should not merely stand on stage in the classic recital position but instead should create the illusion that they were actually doing what the text indicated: he, writing letters to his wife; she, composing an essay about him twenty years after his death. Little by little, pieces of furniture joined the piano on stage: a pair of armchairs, two desks with pen and paper, desk lamps, small carpets. These were arranged, mirror-fashion, flanking the tail of the piano, which was pointed at the audience and acting as a dividing wall between the two singers. In effect, the duocycle became a chamber opera. Performing the work in that manner had never occurred to me, but I had no serious objection.

Earlier, Tyrone Guthrie had mentioned that he felt a bit of staging would not be out of place in *Letters from Composers*. It has been done that way, and some of my other cycles have also been interpreted with a little staging: *Virginia Woolf* and *Miss Manners on Music* have both been performed with the singer seated at a desk, pen in hand. *The Andrée Expedition* has been done as a report to an explorers' society, complete with a slide presentation (using Strindberg's original slides).

I was preoccupied, however, by a completely different and unexpected matter: the use of piano for accompaniment was a serious mistake. I had not taken into consideration the piano's main defect: its inability to sustain long-held chords or single tones; both immediately begin to die out the instant they are struck so that any support for the voice quickly fades away. This was particularly crucial in the slower tempi songs. The correction, I decided, was to redo the piece for a medium-sized orchestra. (At first I thought of using the same ensemble I had used in *A Water Bird Talk* so that they might be performed together, but when this commission materialized, I opted for a somewhat larger instrumentation.)

My decision to orchestrate an accompaniment originally intended for piano has a famous precedent. Berlioz's song cycle *Les nuits d'été* was composed for mezzo with piano accompaniment in 1840 and published in that format. Later he scored one of the songs, "Absence." I think he orchestrated "Absence" because it presented the identical problem I mentioned above, namely, the piano's inability to sustain tones for any length of time, especially in a song as slow-moving as "Absence." Fifteen years after scoring that one song, he seems to have felt the need to orchestrate all the remaining songs of the cycle even though that same problem was not an issue.

I believe his reason for doing so was much the same as mine: in addition to the piano's shortcoming in prolonging sonorities, I realized that its tone was too cold to convey adequately the text I had chosen to set, and I think the same realization may have struck Berlioz. The emotions displayed in both *Nuits d'été* and *A Few Words about Chekhov* call for a much warmer environment than the piano can provide—strings, flutes, horns, harp—something to equal or underline the warmth of the emotions described in these texts. In *From the Diary of Virginia Woolf,* the intimacy and unflinching self-analysis of that text is well matched with the piano's coolness and detachment. (Angel Records, the company that had Janet Baker under contract, was immediately interested in recording the work but not in its original piano version. They offered to undertake a recording if I would orchestrate the work. I told them that the warmer colors of an orchestra would surely spoil the cycle.) And as for *The Andrée Expedition,* it is difficult for me to think of an instrument better qualified than the piano to underscore the white, frozen landscape of the Arctic.

Reverie
(Reflections on a Hymn Tune)
(1997)

∾

Reworking of the organ solo *Prelude for Easter Dawning*
10 minutes
Performed 26 November 1997, Orchestra Hall, Minneapolis,
Minnesota; Eiji Oue, conductor, Minnesota Orchestra

When the Minnesota Orchestra commissioned a ten-minute work to take along on its tour of Europe, I thought of finding and using a tune familiar to most Europeans, one they might follow as it was subjected to continual variations. Believing that a well-known Protestant hymn tune stood a far better chance than any folk song of being recognized in England, Germany, Austria, France, and even in the United States, I fell back on one of my own favorites, the Easter hymn "Ellacombe," which had originally been written for a Catholic service in Württemberg, then became popular with Protestants as well. It also had the advantage that I had used it earlier in the only solo organ work I had ever written, and where I believe it is wasted since that piece isn't among my best works—far from it. Consequently, I took a few decent elements of the organ work and fashioned the orchestral work from them, although the two pieces are only loosely similar.

I had wanted to title the piece *Reflections on a Hymn Tune,* but Asadour Santourian, artistic administrator of the Minnesota Orchestra, who had asked me to write the piece, convinced me to call it *Reverie,* a title I dislike and find highly misleading. To my mind, *reverie* (as in Debussy's piano piece) connotes something static, tranquil, and amorphous, whereas this piece is anything but that. The shape is one extended crescendo from *ppp* to *fff* with occasional interruptions to break the predictability, and the scoring is intended to move from darkness to brightness. Obviously the metaphor intended is a religious one, a progression from doubt and denial to acceptance and conviction.

Two novelties appear in this work. The first happens at a point near the middle of the piece, where only the men seated at the rear of the orchestra (where the audience will not see lips moving) are asked to sing part of the hymn very softly, as if it were coming from a great distance. The other novelty comes at the end. It is one of the very few pieces of mine to have a big finish. The vast majority of my compositions end very, very softly, in some cases as if they were still continuing beyond audibility.

My publisher once told me that orchestra conductors are always on the lookout for contemporary pieces with a duration of about ten minutes because programming such pieces silences those well-disposed critics and listeners who complain that contemporary composers are being ignored. At the same time, a ten-minute work doesn't take up too much valuable rehearsal time the conductor would prefer to spend on polishing Beethoven's Fifth. The relatively frequent performances of *Valentino Dances* (ten minutes and a few seconds) provide a case in point. *Reverie,* however, with an almost identical duration, is rarely programmed.

I attribute the neglect to one thing: the excessively romantic soupiness of an inappropriate title. If I were a conductor browsing through a pile of new scores with an eye to possible performance, it is certain I would not even raise the cover of one titled *Reverie*. I believe a title should provide a hint of what to expect, to welcome the listener into the piece, not lock him out, and I consider it an important matter. In the sixties and seventies, the most opaque titles imaginable were applied to new compositions: *Negative Matrix, Centricity, Relata, Parallax.* I have always felt that such titles, while subtly vouching for the composers' intellectual heft, were the equivalent of posting Keep Out signs on the music, putting listeners off or, worse still, mystifying and ultimately alienating them.

Reverie may not be in that category, but I think it is equally efficient in stimulating indifference. It is regrettable that I did not insist on retaining my original title (which I believe both welcomed the listener into the piece and told what was to be expected) or, at least, restore my title later on. Unfortunately, the latter option was precluded by its becoming known under its present title both from the tour through Europe and, later, by the recording of the work.

Miss Manners on Music
(1998)

∞

Seven songs for mezzo and piano
22 minutes
Newspaper articles by Judith Martin (Miss Manners)
Performed 12 September 1998, Cosmos Club, Washington, D.C.;
 Phyllis Pancella, mezzo; Tim Hoekman, piano

In 1995, three years before this work was premiered, I received a letter from Robert Martin, the husband of Miss Manners, saying that I was his wife's favorite living composer (I had met them both briefly at Wolftrap several years earlier during a performance of *Postcard from Morocco*) and that he wished to celebrate her sixtieth birthday in 1998 with a surprise: a cycle of songs based on excerpts from her advice column. Would I accept such a commission? Thus began a correspondence that would stretch out over twenty months. Although it seemed like a harebrained idea, I didn't want to hurt his feelings, so I begged off by saying I was very busy with an opera that would keep me tied up for the next year or two. Six months later he wrote and asked if I was still tied up. Yes, I was. The following year he wrote again: was I still tied up and, even if so, was there any chance I might somehow fulfill his request before September 1998? This time I attempted to dodge the matter by letting him know that a cycle running some twenty-five minutes could be a very costly birthday present, even for a member of the Esterhazy clan. He was not to be denied. How much? he asked. I quoted him the fairly substantial figure, thinking that would surely frighten him off and end the discussion. Contrary to expectations, he was delighted, agreed to the fee, and sent me four large anthologies of his wife's writings.

Now I was stuck. I browsed through the volumes: articles on the correct behavior to be followed at weddings, funerals, restaurants, theaters. I hastily scanned all these with a sinking heart, trying to invent still another excuse to pull out of the semicommitment I had unwittingly gotten myself into, when I came across one of her columns giving advice on how to behave at the ballet. Unlike her famous predecessors, such as Emily Post, Miss Manners's counsel is light-hearted, delightful, and witty. Gradually an idea began to coalesce, and I searched the more than one thousand pages thoroughly until I found what I hoped might be there: advice on how to behave at the opera, at the symphony, at a concert of contemporary music, at a church recital, and so on. After I assembled and studied a possible text consisting of seven excerpts, my interest began to waken to the task, and by the time I started composing the music I was enthusiastic about the project. As is always the case, once the text was right, composition went rapidly.

The premiere itself was a memorable occasion. Mr. Martin arranged for us to arrive several days early (in order to rehearse, secretly, with Ms. Pancella and her pianist), putting us up at Washington's exclusive Cosmos Club, the local favorite with newspaper people—one wall is completely covered with hundreds of photos of Pulitzer Prize winners. (We were entertained at the club years before by Paul Hume, music critic for the *Washington Post,* during a Kennedy Center revival of *Postcard from Morocco* in which Hume's son had a role.) At 3 p.m. on Miss Manners's birthday, one hundred and fifty of her friends and colleagues gathered in the ballroom. Printed programs had been placed on all the chairs beforehand. Miss Manners was aware that a party had been organized but did not know that a new cycle commissioned in her honor was about to be unveiled. It had remained a secret from her and most of the guests. Her husband escorted her into the ballroom to a standing ovation from the guests. The surprise was almost spoiled when she reached for the program on her chair. Mr. Martin quickly confiscated it and distracted her by pointing to where Carolyn and I were seated: our presence there must have seemed surprising to her, but it did not give anything away. All was revealed when the ballroom doors opened again and Miss Manners's favorite singer—Phyllis Pancella—and pianist entered and went over to the grand piano on the small stage. Phyllis gave a truly hilarious performance that was warmly received by all and followed by a very well mannered English high tea.

The Vision
(1999)

∞

Motet for mixed chorus and string quartet
7 minutes
Excerpts from the Paradise section of *The Divine Comedy* by Dante
    Alighieri
Performed 17 June 2000, Church of the Transfiguration,
    Orleans, Cape Cod, Massachusetts; Elizabeth Patterson,
    conductor, Gloriæ Dei Cantores

The Gloriæ Dei Cantores is a superb choral group composed primarily of amateurs devoted both to singing and to a religious community based on Cape Cod. I was told they leave their jobs for three months each year to practice, give concerts, and record. A few years previous to this composition I received in the mail one of their CDs, which included my *Easter Day.* To my great surprise, their performance was exquisite. A bit later they issued a box CD set covering four hundred years of American choral music, which concluded with my *Let All the World in Every Corner Sing,* and it too was beautifully done. Their community planned to build a new church as their permanent center, to open in the spring of 2000. The formal opening of the edifice would be an elaborate affair, and I was commissioned to compose an inaugural work.

The contract specified that the text should have something to do with an account of Christ's Transfiguration, and I was kindly supplied with chapter and verse of all the places in the Bible where that miracle is described. I checked out the passages and found the descriptions strangely pithy, usually a single sentence or two, offering precious little for a composer to work with. I decided I had better look elsewhere. Luckily I remembered the passage in the Paradise section of Dante's *Divine Comedy* when Beatrice takes Dante to see Christ. That description of a transfigured Christ, unlike those of the apostles, is spectacular, vivid, and majestic. I joined a few sections that were not sequential in the original and added the *Commedia*'s amazing closing lines. I had expected to go to Cape Cod for the opening ceremonies, but the occasion coincided with the onset of my medical *via dolorosa.* To this day, I have never heard the piece performed live but have had several warm letters from people who have heard and praised it. It was a joy to set Dante's text at last, especially after years of brooding about what I might do with his *La vita nuova.*

Nicolas Nabokov was at work on a setting of *La vita nuova* when we parted ways in 1951 (according to *The New Grove Dictionary of Music and Musicians,* it was also performed that year—in Europe, I guess—although I've never heard a word about it). The idea that I also might set Dante's account of his meeting with Beatrice has remained with me ever since, and from time to time, when a commission seemed suitable, I have considered various ways of going about it, but it remains my great unwritten piece. The text is marvelously suited for musical treatment. In it, there are a number of poems about Dante's first encounter with his beloved. In between these sections, in prose, he explains the conceits and hidden meanings of the poems.

Sometimes I planned on composing it for a single singer; sometimes for two. Sometimes I considered having a single ensemble accompany both singers; sometimes one singer would be accompanied by a smallish group, the other singer with full orchestra. Sometimes I thought the whole piece would be entirely in Italian or in English;

sometimes I thought of leaving the poems in Italian and translating the prose explanations into English (obviously the macaronic version appealed to me most of all). This last arrangement, with soprano and chamber ensemble for the poems (in Italian) and tenor and full orchestra for the prose (in English), was the closest to my ideal version, but it never got done. The problem was duration. Dante's work consists of thirty poems, and—when set to music—a performance would take as long as an uncut *Hamlet*, too great an imposition on any listener, I feared. Editing it down to even an hour's duration (a maximum, I felt) meant omitting so much that when I tried, I lost my nerve.

The Bremen Town Musicians
(1999)

∾

Entertainment for children with narrator and orchestra
23 minutes
Fairy tale by the Brothers Grimm
Performed 11 April 2000, Kennedy Center, Washington, D.C.;
    Stephen Simon, conductor, Washington Chamber
    Symphony

At the party following the premiere of *Miss Manners on Music,* Judith Martin grew very enthusiastic about collaborating on an opera for children. I said of course I'd be interested as long as the libretto appealed to me. She and her husband left for their annual Venetian vacation during which I received a number of e-mails from Robert telling me he had never seen Judith work so hard: the libretto had become an obsession. When I finally received a complete act I and a synopsis of the second act, my heart sank. It was not at all what I had hoped it might be. Telling Judith that the ideas did not work for me was most difficult, and with that our friendship, which I had truly enjoyed, temporarily sank out of sight.

The Bremen Town Musicians went through something similar. I was commissioned to write a piece that would appeal to young audiences, à la *Peter and the Wolf.* After a disappointing rummage through the usual fairy and folk tale literature, it occurred to me to approach Garrison Keillor to see if he might be interested in a collaboration. Yes, he would. Soon I received an e-mail from him laying out a possible synopsis. The idea was a peculiar take (including doo-wop and other hip elements) on *Little Red Riding Hood.* No doubt his readership and radio audience would have found it vastly entertaining, but I wasn't sure anyone younger than nine years of age would find it amusing.

Not wishing to hurt his feelings or be insulting, I didn't want to say it was hopeless, but I did ask if perhaps he had any other ideas. He would see. Several days later, he came up with an autobiographical idea: having recently become a parent, he concocted something about a father awakened in the middle of the night, his heart pierced by the wailing of his infant daughter (a sound he claimed as heart-rending as anything Puccini had ever dreamed up); details about changing her diaper (which was rhymed with "don't forget to wipe her"); and so forth. Having turned down his first idea, I didn't have the face to rudely refuse his second effort, and so I looked for an excuse to back out of our collaborative endeavor. In a week or two I'd be leaving for Italy, I explained, where I needed to begin composing the music. Knowing he had a number of projects going on at that time, I said I'd like to have the finished script in hand before we left: would he be able to give me the complete text by then? No, he didn't work that way: he liked to keep things fluid, revising, changing direction, improvising right up to the last minute, so he'd prefer to use e-mail to send me ideas, scenes, revisions, and cuts in Florence as the music was being written. Our work methods were utterly incompatible (he called mine "having all your ducks in a row," which is indeed a very accurate description). That being the case, we abandoned the idea of collaboration. Under different circumstances, I believe we might have been able to produce something interesting, and I truly regret that nothing came of this aborted effort: had there been no time constraints, I would gladly have humored him longer until he hit upon a subject I might find more sympathetic and suitable.

In the end I chose *The Bremen Town Musicians,* the same Grimm's fairy tale Bernard Rogers had once made into a tone poem. (He had a genuine love of fairy tales and had turned a number of them into charming musical works.) I adapted the story myself, converting it into a kind of theatrical concerto grosso for four solo instruments and orchestra. I also tacked on a moral for children: practice (music practice in this case) makes perfect. Considering that it was a quick makeshift alternative after the disappointment with Keillor, the work came out much better than I had any right to expect, and I feel it was a much wiser choice in the long run, an opinion, I believe, that the enthusiasm of the young audience at the premiere reinforced.

Sonnet 64
(In memoriam 9/11/01)
(2001)

∾

Motet for unaccompanied chorus
4 minutes
Poetry by William Shakespeare
Performed 10 August 2002, Orchestra Hall, Minneapolis,
    Minnesota; Boris Teslov, conductor, Moscow Conservatory
    Chorus

My publisher asked me for a program note that would be printed in the score of this piece. It reads: "We were living in Florence when terrorists attacked the twin towers of the World Trade Center. A friend of mine and manager of St. Paul's Schubert Club, Bruce Carlson, e-mailed Sonnet 64 to me, saying he had wished to reprint the poem in their booklet for an upcoming recital but his office staff, finding it too bleak, talked him out of it. I agreed with his staff, but his e-mail was pure serendipity to me: not having yet found a text for the short choral piece commissioned by the Sixth World Symposium on Choral Music, Shakespeare's poem so perfectly accorded with my own response to the events of 9/11 that this brief elegy virtually wrote itself."

I am realizing now for the first time just how little Shakespeare I have actually set to music even though not a year has gone by that

I didn't contemplate doing something with one of the poems or plays. (I do not count *Christopher Sly,* much of which is not really Shakespeare at all, due to the incompleteness of the original and the heavy adaptation it underwent.) Two of his poems were included in *Six Elizabethan Songs. Variations for Orchestra* is based on quotations from various plays, but only one of Juliet's speeches is actually set to music. Only one other setting of a Shakespeare text joined them, and that after the passage of almost forty years. (Oddly enough, all of these pieces were written in Florence; *Sonnet 64* was composed in our most recent Florence address, via delle Belle Donne 15, the street on which the Brownings lived—prior to their Casa Guidi residence—when they first arrived in the city.)

During those intervening four decades, I frequently browsed through the plays and toyed with various operatic possibilities but gave serious and prolonged consideration to only two: *Love's Labours Lost* and *The Comedy of Errors.* Of the former, I was convinced that a perceptive, elegant score could nicely enhance the play's sensibilities and lyricism. (In 1973, Berlin's Deutsche Oper premiered Nabokov's *Love's Labours Lost,* a collaboration with the librettists of *The Rake's Progress:* W. H. Auden and Chester Kallman. The *New Grove Dictionary* describes it as cast in an eclectic parody style *"the composer called 'persiflage,' sending up Tristan and Beethoven's Fifth Symphony in Berowne's love aria, Weill and Eisler in the 'Discourse About Love', American crooning in Moth's songs, Glinka and Mussorgsky . . . and catches and madrigals passim."*)

About *The Comedy of Errors,* I felt that—of all the plays—it ran the least risk of being damaged by music. The sheer grandeur of *Hamlet, Macbeth,* and *The Tempest* placed them beyond the bounds of my deliberations. Those three masterpieces have been the cause of countless operatic shipwrecks, including one by Verdi himself. (I discount the persistent rumor that Mozart, close to the end of his life, was thinking of an opera based on *The Tempest.* However unbelievable that may be, just the thought of it makes me smile.) I think operas based on any one of that trio of sirens are doomed to failure because the language and images are so rich that the addition of music can do nothing but make them cloying. It was brilliant of Verdi (in his old age) to choose precisely the right plays to adapt: *Otello,* which many critics agree is an improvement over *Othello*; and *Falstaff,* the sum of whose parts is much greater than the whole.

The one Elizabethan play I most regret not having turned into an opera is Ben Jonson's *Bartholomew Fair.* I had long wished to make a great, sprawling comic opera of it but kept putting it off for a later time. And now that the later time has come, unfortunately I lack the energy such a huge undertaking would require. Another Shakespeare (actually semi-Shakespeare) project that I returned to time and again was a cantata based on *The Passionate Shepherd* for soprano, mezzo, and tenor: she, the narrator, and he. As was the case with *La vita nuova,* the text would have had to be shortened to make its duration manageable, and cutting up the poetry of even questionable Shakespeare is not done lightly.

Orpheus
(2002)

∾

Short piece for treble voices (SSA) a cappella
6 minutes
Poetry by Sir Osbert Sitwell
Performed 27 April 2003, Ninety-second Street Y, New York
    City, New York; Francisco Nuñez, conductor, Young
    People's Chorus

This is the first (and may perhaps be the only) work I have composed using a computer. During our annual stays in Florence I have always rented a piano. For years its delivery (very often up seven flights of stairs) was accomplished by three burly gentlemen and a much smaller and older man who I assumed to be their father. Their procedure never varied: the little fellow, doubled over, carried the full weight of the upright piano on his back; two of the other men steadied the ends of the piano, one in front and one behind to keep it from tipping over, while the fourth acted as cheerleader (providing encouragement with cries of "Forza!" and "Coraggio!") and guide, warning of approaching turns, switching on the stairwell's timed lights whenever they went off, and so on. The same technique was also used when the piano was removed from our apartment and appeared to be even more precarious when employed in the downward direction.

The fact that *Orpheus* is a relatively simple piece is what allowed me to compose at the computer. In anything calling for a denser texture or more complex harmonies, I have to refer frequently to the piano. In this case, the music was silently notated on the computer's screen (using a Finale software program), generally in sections of eight or ten measures at a time, then played back, either through the computer's built-in speakers or a tiny earphone, to check—since I am not blessed with perfect pitch—if what I wrote was what I wanted to hear. The earphone method allowed Carolyn, for the first time, to sit reading or writing in the same room where I was composing. (I have always disliked having anyone in the same room when I needed to work at the piano.)

There are both advantages and disadvantages to composing with the computer: when the composer is satisfied with the work, there is no need to make a fair copy because the computer's perfectly engraved version can be published as it stands. But there is also a very negative concomitant: no sketches or early drafts exist. All improvements simply replace the original material; consequently, future musicologists will be unable to reconstruct the development of a work through the progression of its sketches. A greater loss is that no calligraphic manuscripts, like Bach's elegant hand or Beethoven's spiky one, remain behind.

As this catalogue is being compiled, *Orpheus* is the last entry. Should it turn out to be my last composition, that would not be inappropriate since the first thing publicly performed in my undergraduate years (at a composers' forum where an unmarried Carolyn sang in our ad hoc chorus) was a set of three a cappella pieces not unlike this one. That little cycle takes its text from Rabindranath Tagore's *Gitanjali (Prayer Offerings)*. Its opening lines are prophetic:

I am here to sing thee songs.
In this house of thine I have a corner seat.
In thy world I have no work to do.
My useless life can only break out
in tunes without a purpose.

Even the notes to which the initial words "I am here" are set—
A, B-flat, C—are prophetic: that musical cell (a half step followed by
a whole step) I now recognize as being my musical fingerprint, and
it shows up prominently in almost everything I have ever written.
I became aware of its ubiquity only a few years ago when it simultaneously dawned on me that the same tiny cell begins the slow section
of Gershwin's *Rhapsody in Blue,* a work that had a great influence in my
adolescence.

In my end is my beginning. These pages span more than half a century of
doing the thing I've loved most. The amount of time separating the
composition of *Orpheus* from *Songs about Spring* seems very brief to me,
yet it is exactly the same as that separating my birth from the premiere of the opera *Carmen,* which seems shrouded in the mists of history. It scarcely seems possible that such a great period of time could
have elapsed since a youngster in knickers first entered a brand-new
public library and discovered an astounding world of books and
music. Were it not for the five dozen pieces of music catalogued
here, I could easily believe it was only last year.

From a Composer's Journal

∽

The following passages are taken from a diary I kept during the composition of *The Voyage of Edgar Allan Poe.* The diary was never meant to be published; it was intended to serve as a personal record of the compositional experience and as a reminder in later years of how the work progressed from idea to reality—something I am always unable to recall with earlier pieces of mine.

In November 1975 I read portions of the journal to an audience of National Opera Association members. Some of them urged me to make the diary available. I have agreed to do so, providing the text appears exactly as first written, faults and all, without altering or polishing it. If an occasional remark seems somewhat self-congratulatory (as others may seem self-critical), I can only defend their inclusion by admitting that I want the diary to reflect my thoughts and moods at the time the entries were composed. Modesty might suggest discreet editing, but doing so would falsify the account and diminish what little value these remarks may possess as an accurate record. Any deleted sections and omissions are portions I consider to be of no interest to anyone but myself or are of a purely private nature beyond the scope of this present purpose.

January 13, 1974

Sometime before Christmas, Frank Sorauf (dean of the College of Liberal Arts, University of Minnesota) broached the idea of the University commissioning an opera for the Bicentennial. Almost two years ago, in Florence, I came upon Thornton Wilder's "Heaven's My Destination" and felt strongly it would make an ideal Bicentennial work if a commission ever materialized. I continued to think about it believing it might just be a gentle, American "Wozzeck" sort of work. My only doubt centered on the necessarily naturalistic treatment the novel would demand . . . This past Monday or Tuesday—still worrying about the realistic element—it occurred to me that perhaps something could be done with the Tales of E. A. Poe, something fantastic and nonrealistic. The idea developed like this:

1) Maybe several short tales related around a single theme;
2) that brought to mind "Tales of Hoffmann";
3) perhaps a frame around the Tales with Poe himself a character;
4) reading Poe's biography, I discovered the mysterious manner of his death: boarding a steamer at Richmond, he was found unconscious in a gutter in Baltimore one week later and died shortly thereafter—the intervening six or seven days (aboard the steamer) have never been accounted for;
5) within that framework (the mysterious voyage) several tales could be worked—all of it treated fancifully and fictionally: a possible title: "The Murder of Edgar Allan Poe."

I'll meet with Charles Nolte next Friday to get his reaction: his play about Strindberg is somewhat like the scheme I have in mind.

January 18

Lunched today with Nolte and explained my ideas about a Poe opera. He is fascinated by the locale—the packet-boat—and the possible variety of characters, especially Poe himself. His enthusiasm confirms my own conviction. He will begin "thinking" about it.

January 24

Been reading much Poe and criticism and becoming increasingly enthused about the possibilities. The important thing now is that the libretto be just right.

February 9

Duality should operate on several levels, if it doesn't confuse matters: The characters, so far, are

Poe (tenor)
Griswold (baritone)
Virginia (soprano)
Annie (mezzo)
Narrator (bass?)

Annie is a composite of all the women Poe courted (Sarah, Elmira, Helen, Frances, etc.). Perhaps her name should be Helen. Each real character equates with one of Poe's fictional creations:

Poe—Roderick Usher
Virginia—Madelaine Usher (sister)
Griswold—William Wilson (Imp of the Perverse)
Annie/Helen—Ligeia
Narrator—Captain Hardy/Dupin?

Furthermore, Poe = Griswold

Virginia = Annie

Too fancy???

Also, I wonder whether any Tales should appear complete? Or only characters and incidents from them? I hope I can begin to discuss this next week with Nolte. Left to myself, ideas merely continue to float around in air.

February 19

Charles to lunch yesterday. We had a first lengthy talk—or monologue—on the opera. I gave him five typed pages of notes and suggestions. All of them seemingly acceptable to him.

May 5

Almost two month lapse here. I'm definitely not the diarist type. Yesterday the "Woolf" cycle was completed. Despite my feeling at the outset on March 27 that I would compose slowly and stretch it out, the eight songs were completed in just over five weeks, and—I think, now at least—they are the best vocal writing I've done. Probably because the text is the best I've ever worked with: each song was sketched out in two or three days with only one or two false starts among the collection. I think this is because the mood in each excerpt is so pure and clear, private and simple. How ideal for opera, but I don't imagine V. W. would have plotted well enough for anything of that length. I must see that the Poe libretto concludes on an "emotional" note—don't exactly know what I mean, though. It seems to me that the best quality in "Letters," "Postcard" and now "Woolf" is the emotional impact they carry; it seems my strongest point. And when I think over the ends of "Mask of Night," "Bravo Mozart!" and especially "Ring of Time" I see it is part of my ritual to go for poignant conclusions, usually pianissimo.

May 27

Tomorrow I send "Woolf" songs to Boosey & Hawkes and on to Janet Baker. I wonder if she will "react" to them. I notice this diary says nothing about the composition of that diary! On May 15th. N.E.A. renewed the grant for my own libretto of the Chekhov monologue.

Since Charles still needs the summer to write the Poe text, I'll start the monodrama next. It is strange, though, to be writing a piece with no performance or occasion in mind. Frankly, I wish I were starting the Poe: the idea of beginning in September with only 12 months for a full-length piece is a bit tight.

October 3

At the rate things are entered in this diary, this little volume could last a lifetime. The previous entry speaks about the completion of the song cycle. I began the N.E.A. monodrama sometime after that (end of June?) and finished it in vocal score last week—not a word is written here. The timing was just right: tomorrow I meet with Nolte to see his efforts on the Poe opera. I can't imagine what he'll have. He's been slower than I expected. Luckily, the Chekhov has kept me occupied. The monodrama has turned out well, I think. It was a very concentrated two or three months of work and, as a result, seems very tight to me—compact and rich, highly organized and yet free-ranging. Certainly the best crack at characterization I've made— probably as a result of coming fresh from "Woolf." As much as I think the Chekhov works (now titled "A Water Bird Talk"), I hope to make the Poe still freer, more adventurous—but can I? Does one really have any control over these things? Just two weeks ago, approaching the end of the monodrama, I decided to dawdle over the ending—try out various things. But instead, the last ten minutes or so were sketched out effortlessly in a single day. So effortlessly that I thought it wouldn't stand and I spent a week trying to improve on it, only to find that the original idea worked best. (Verdi's: "Art without spontaneity is lifeless.") Perhaps now, with a libretto in sight, this notebook will gather less dust.

October 7

Saturday last, at 3 p.m., Charles read to me Act I of the Poe opera (and snippets of Act II). A great disappointment, leaving me much depressed. By today I had hoped to be starting the music: as it is, we are starting the libretto again tomorrow! His first act—(odd, that he went ahead and wrote it all without the conferences we had discussed: he indicated to me that I would see trial scenes and several possible scenarios—instead Act I was *fait accompli,* turned out to be as long as "Götterdämmerung" and twice as gloomy. All metaphysical talk and rhetoric—Poe on stage continuously, forever singing arias, and I think I counted half-a-dozen duets for Poe and Griswold. During the past 48 hours I've been trying to salvage something from the text. Certain scenes are fine, but I've recast the whole scenario and emphasis.

After doing this, I consulted the five or six pages of notes I gave Charles months ago: I see that my re-working agrees 100% with those notes, making me wonder if Charles ever looked at them. Still, I think something may yet come of this, but this is my first time playing the role Puccini always played with his librettists. Charles comes tomorrow and we will go over my new 10 pages of notes. I've set up seven scenes and sketched out roughly what goes on in each. I feel strange telling a teacher of playwrighting how to construct a drama, but, where libretti are concerned, I have some experience, and I do know my own strengths (what I *can* set to music and what I can't). No doubt Charles will accept my views, but will he bring about what I *mean?* This subject, above most others, means walking a very fine line between the serious and the melodramatic, the imaginative and the silly, the profound and the pompous.

October 8

Charles here between 4 and 6 p.m. I spent this morning and early afternoon reviewing and refining my notes for Charles. As I did so, my enthusiasm was revived—(the shape and tone are back where I want them without too much violence to Charles' script, although more than half was discarded. Keeping the spine of six of his scenes, it is possible to alter the tone and—like V. Woolf—I saw the fin again, out in the distant sea—far out, but at least it is the fish I hoped to net.

It occurred to me during the revisions that I might have done the libretto myself. I am pleased with the monodrama, but I lack the confidence to tackle anything as ambitious as Poe. And yet, in the revising, I could see the entire Poe very clearly—but perhaps this is only because I had Charles' first draft to build on, as I had the Chekhov to build on. I feel that Act I will work very well. Act II remains a question mark. Perhaps it will have to undergo a transformation similar to Act I.

October 31

On the 13th (Sunday) Charles brought the revised Act I much, much improved except for the finale, which he is re-doing. (Strange: although he incorporated most of my suggestions, he ignored my ideas for this finale. But his is equally good, although I need some changes.)

It is still too long. I've cut almost one-fifth (on my own). In any case, I began the music on October 14: Columbus Day—an auspicious time to launch this "voyage of discovery," I hope.

So far, about ten minutes of music. In the first six minutes, only percussion is used: the next four minutes uses only strings and a few woodwind touches. I want to save the full orchestra for the arrival of the ship. Also, at this point, I want to pause and think about both libretto and score a bit more.

The music must have a point of view—instrumental colors, motifs, etc., not fully thought out yet. (Griswold is about to arrive on stage and I think the problem now arises for individual music.)

The libretto still bothers me. Is it only a fanciful biography of Poe? Somehow, the fantastic element isn't as strong as I envisioned and Poe's works (the tales, poems) are peripheral rather than central. I must look at it again for variety and a certain amount of madness. It seems too sane, too logical. Perhaps I must read it to some outsiders for reaction: I keep comparing it to the imaginary script I long ago concocted (the fin) and find the present script wanting. But it is very difficult to say where the discrepancy lies. Rather like pieces of music I imagine before writing them: the "ideal" is so much richer and freer than the final result. Putting anything down on paper somehow impoverishes the mental picture. Maybe this has always been so. I will suspend judgment until Charles brings Act II.

November 15

Scene II virtually done.

Yesterday's workout was extremely productive. I could barely write fast enough to catch all the ideas. It took 16 hours to copy out my scribbles of yesterday morning. It also produced a sleepless night (ideas churning) and a slightly feverish condition—at least a headache.

Gradually, the piece is coming into focus: it *is* turning into the work I hoped it would be. Griswold certainly is a fascinating character: Poe, being the tenor, has less character, but better tunes.

December 15

One month since the last entry. At that time, I thought the "Quintet" was practically finished, but it nagged at me for another two weeks and became finally a "Septet" with chorus, intentionally modeled on the "Lucia" Sextet—very grand scale. It ought to be fine, but it was a lot of work.

Yesterday I almost completed Scene III (the quarrel with Allan, his father by adoption)—a week's work. It is a mad gallop and rises to a nice climax, *alla quintetto,* for Poe's declaration. It has a whirlwind pace and should run about three minutes. Another deliberate model are those breathless trios in "Aida" and "Trovatore."

About 10 days ago. Bob Moore said, "I hope your opera is a romantic one." Without thinking about it, I said it will be my middle Verdi opera *alla* "Rigoletto" or, really "Trovatore," which it most resembles in its darkness (night eternal), melodrama, *terribilità.* After saying this, I realized that that had been my intention from the outset, though never articulated. "Poe" is so very 1849, it *has* to be Verdi. (Before actually realizing this, the early part of Scene II—the "melo-drama" of Mrs. Poe's death—I set as almost a parody of Donizetti-Bellini-early Verdi.) Yesterday was the three-month mark since I started composing: I must be just about in the middle of Act I. Exactly on schedule.

December 24

Finished the Rowboat scene this morning—a week's work for six minutes of music. I think it ought to be enchanting. Really a trio, quite simple and tender for Poe and Virginia, and quietly ominous for Griswold. I hope it comes off as understated as I wish: I was going to avoid any climax (to contrast the bracketing scenes) but I couldn't resist just one *forte* measure where it flashes by in a long sweeping crescendo-decrescendo. The orchestration is better than I hoped—nice woodwind and harp touches—no brass save horns—and mostly low strings for the boat-rocking effect. The character of Virginia comes out clearly (to me).

I only wish Act II libretto were finished . . . it worries me that I've come this far without a clearer notion of events in Act II. It must not, in any event, be a letdown or weakening. And I still want a lump-in-the-throat welling up of sympathy for the pitiful life Poe had. That, after all, is the point of dragging on stage the grotesque episodes of his biography. It must *account* for him.

January 20, 1975

Charles just left. Last Friday he brought two-thirds of Act II. Good things in it, but all wrong for my purposes: the first three or four scenes were all gloom. All the following ones were peaks. I spent the weekend—in the same low spirits I had after seeing the first act draft—trying to salvage the work. This entailed doing a new finale to Act I which I hope will be a great improvement, and rearranging Act II material. The second death of Virginia came as an inspiration and ought to be a most thrilling scene, carrying the "Resurrection" beyond being a mere *coup de théâtre*.

Also, I had to weed out more metaphysical chatter: The difficulty for a dramatist-turned-librettist . . . is realizing how unimportant words are, how dull rational dialogue is in opera. In any case, I believe the scenario is right now for Act II, only it must not run on too long. I am in the middle of the Wedding Scene now. It got off to a good start last week.

February 5

Just put finishing touches on the Wedding Scene. What a lot of hard work it has been! Most of January was spent on it . . . it runs 60 pages for 10 minutes of music. I hope the hard effort doesn't show—that it doesn't emerge as lifeless or belabored.

The next brief scene must be short and unmusical—recitative with piano and percussion most likely—to set the ground for the finale.

February 28

I stop in the middle of a section that is going very well this morning to enter a few words of apology for whatever doubts I've had about Nolte's libretto. Often in Act I, I've ignored his arrangement to improvise something better, only to return in the end to his original version. After finding the musical solution for it I discover it is really superior to my own makeshift. The section that is going so well is Poe's "Boston Lecture" in the finale—I think the big lyric statement here caps the scene (and Act) emotionally. Thank heavens we expanded it to allow the tune!

The only problem Act I poses anymore is the drinking ensemble and—more especially—how to end when Virginia appears. The close is the most difficult matter—no grand guignol, but still very exciting and thrilling. Perhaps by mid-March I'll finish: a precise five months for the first Act.

March 22

I put the finishing touches to Act I this morning. The finale was more difficult than I thought: I don't believe I've ever worked so hard and intensely before. I also believe it may be the most thrilling scene I've ever tried. . . .

March 25

Charles brought the last two scenes yesterday. Actually, three of four scenes—a completely unexpected and unwelcome cemetery scene. And as per pattern, I was completely dejected—not at all what I expected or wanted. And. again, per pattern, with some juggling around, re- or de-emphasis, I found an order to make it possible, but it requires recasting half of the Act, particularly the opening. This, I'm afraid, means a delay beginning the Act II music. Charles came this morning to hear my reaction and, obliging as ever, he will re-cast it as I like. He agrees that my tightening does improve things. It also cuts more philosophical chatter and emphasizes the Orpheus-Eurydice myth in the background.

April 21

Almost a month since the last entry. A month of serious doubts about the work. A hard time getting started on the second act and a depressed feeling that Act I wasn't as good as I thought it was earlier. No doubt the two matters are one, really. Several days ago (after almost three weeks niggling at Poe's "Dream Aria"), when the aria began to fall into place, the first Act began to look better again. And when I played through it last week, all my earlier enthusiasm was restored.

May 4

Friday, Charles brought the revised second act. I am now content with it and will probably follow it closely. The overall shape and structure are fine now, I think: interesting, varied, several clear levels of meaning. Still no title. 'The —— Voyage of Edgar Allan Poe." Or perhaps omit the blank (left for an appropriate adjective).

May 23

Finally, (I think) decided on a title: "The Voyage of Edgar Poe." Discarding the adjective before voyage and dropping the middle name. The trial scene is pretty well sketched out. Another day or so should finish it. It seems to be more interesting musically than I thought it would. The idea dropped in Griswold's Arioso—the major/minor sequence for "anima/nemesis" gave the clue for the rest of the scene. So, perhaps I will have about two weeks of work on Virginia's Death Scene before leaving for Europe—if we go at all.

May 27

Trial scene is finished: 19' 30" to this point. Now I feel well into the second act. My main concern is to find something interesting for the Auction Scene. The two scenes with Virginia—death and resurrection—don't bother me at all; those I know I can handle. But the Auction Scene is quite different from anything I've tried before. I'd like it to be both grotesque and comic-burlesque and bizarre. I wish I didn't have to compose it in our Florence apartment—*con sordino,* closed windows (to avoid irritating the neighbors) in summertime: it obviously is going to require banging and thumping. I ought to skip it until we return to Minneapolis, but I can never quite do that: I need to approach works in order, scene by scene, to get the proper flow. Even song cycles get composed that way.

July 13

(Sunday afternoon on the terrace of via dei Bardi 58)

Today begins the second month of our Florentine summer. It has been idyllic, very social and pleasant, and yet—contrary to my apprehension—very productive: except as far as this diary is concerned. I am clearly *not* a diarist. (This and the remaining excerpts are written on loose sheets of paper: the diary had been forgotten back in the U.S.) During the past month I've often thought I must not let this Italian sojourn interrupt the Poe journal after it is already three-quarters complete. But given the choice of spending a few minutes at the desk or the piano, the latter always wins . . . The opera itself is becoming an obsession. Since arriving, I've done Virginia's death scene, partially sketched out before leaving the States, but greatly elaborated here. I suspect it will be the loveliest scene in the work: being in Florence where we once saw "Eurydice" and "Dafne" (two of the earliest operas, written at the beginning of the 17th century in Florence) reminded me of the echo choruses and so the choral lament for Virginia uses the device . . .

The Auction—now half finished—was the single scene that most worried me. It ought to be grotesque and wild—not my strongest suits, I fear. I'm compromising by trying it burlesque and strange and somewhat broadly parodistic, but it may be the wrong track. I just don't know. It's turned into a little divertissement, like Act Two of the Nutcracker—with curious vignettes of the various women. The hard part comes just now where the scene must be transformed into a wild hallucination.

Despite my vow to Charles, I *am* asking for one more change— the pivotal scene where Poe stabs Griswold. At present, Griswold receives the blows, welcomes them, and continues to speak as though nothing happened. I really think, as in "William Wilson," Poe must see that in stabbing Griswold, he is killing himself. Hence, Griswold must be transformed into a blood-covered image of Poe himself, face-to-face with himself before the blackout.

July 15

I must record here two oddities: after the usual arguments about astrology, ESP, etc., with Renata, and my usual skeptical replies . . . Yesterday morning, waiting for friends on the terrace of the Lungarno Hotel, I walked to the river's edge thinking of Virginia's resurrection aria: "Where gold and silver fish swim through the river of silence" . . . Looking down into the Arno, I saw a whole school of goldfish, large ones (six or seven inches), chasing one another and cavorting. I've never seen goldfish in rivers, nor have my friends.

That same afternoon, I added a footnote to the vocal score of "Poe" to attribute the text of "The Dying Rosebud's Lament" to its authoress, Mrs. Frances Sargent Osgood, and suddenly saw my own unusual name leap out at me: Francess *argento* sgood. A simple cryptographic device Poe knew of—transposing the first letter of a word to the tail of the preceding one. Signs and symbols, as John Olon would say, but good or bad?

August 1

Except for a few finishing touches, the Auction Scene is done: the hardest bit of composing I've ever done. Grueling work. and all to create a sense of chaos. A few days ago I sketched out a truly chaotic scene, à la Berio's "Sinfonia"—frantic tempo, some talking, some sprechstimme, several different arias, Yankee Doodle (in a madhouse scene, Poe refers to the bizarre orchestra playing Yankee Doodle in different keys and tempi at one time), and the kitchen sink. The next day I threw it all out. I would truly like to do something outrageous like that, but I always have second thoughts and doubts after trying it. Somehow, it's too easy to create that kind of musical mud. I invariably give it up and find a musical solution. As Mozart wrote to his father of "Abduction": "Even when depicting terrible scenes, the music must still remain music, not mere noise."

August 14

The first real rain in 70 days here.

The Resurrection Scene was finished last week. It took perhaps two weeks, being essentially a recitative for Poe and Griswold, the aria for V. and concluding recitative for the men. I hope V's aria will be the emotional high spot of the opera. It is the demonstration of

Poe's unholy inspiration and poignant use of his only love story (Eleonora). And it should be perfect for Carolyn. Work was accomplished even though Nolte and a friend visited for a few days, followed by the Brunelles for three nights.

The trial scene is resumed and should go quickly once I get a decent idea for it . . . The important thing will be Poe's defense aria. I must admit here to a great sense of weariness—it has been unrelenting work since last October 15th—10 months, day after day of 12 or more hours with only occasional breaks of three or four days. Does it show in the music, I wonder??

September 6

(Our 21st wedding anniversary.) The rains last mentioned have remained these past two weeks. It seems that earlier in this diary (I don't have the book here) I wrote that the end of "A Water Bird Talk" came all in a rush—much faster than I expected it to take. The same thing has happened with "Poe." The 10th scene (what I've always regarded as the real finale) went very rapidly—not even two weeks and I could easily finish the last scene (Epilogue) in 24 hours if I had to. I wonder if this acceleration toward the end is simply a matter of being so saturated with the material; ideas come so easily, or is it a subconscious wish to bring a long labor to an end?

I think the scene (Trial) works well. Poe's defense is an interesting, almost free-form aria, held together by a two-bar refrain (like "Nevermore").

By Thursday, when Tanya [Moiseiwitsch, the designer] arrives it ought to be finished, but no doubt I will tinker with the music until I deliver it to the copyist at the end of this month.

September 11

In two hours, Tanya arrives from London. The opera was finished yesterday, right on schedule, although I've altered a few minor things today and will no doubt continue to do so until we leave.

As usual, with an opera at this stage, there is little sense of satisfaction. I write "finished"; but, of course, there is still the orchestration to do—months of tedious manual and eyestraining work; since the orchestration is already "set" in mind and clearly marked in the vocal score, this is routine labor. "Finished" doesn't mean anything until the dress rehearsals are done. Only then, just prior to the premiere, does the work seem to be completely out of my hands and truly finished.

Also, per usual, after drawing the final double-bar, my thoughts go immediately to all the ideas that never found their way into the work. Those tantalizing possibilities that existed when the work was in the planning stage and early days. Those ideas remain homeless (or perhaps they find homes in later works?) and now I begin to reconsider the options I had. But without discarding some of them, some of their replacements would never have occurred and, in many cases, these second thoughts turned out better than expected.

On balance. What do *I* think of the work at this moment? It is far and away the most ambitious thing I've done; it is fairly close to what I planned it to be (the fin); Verdian, lyric, exciting, imaginative and interesting (to me, naturally), *rich,* in short, which is what I've always wanted for it. I suppose it is less fantastic, less strange than I had hoped. Or am I discovering that many of the fanciful things I can contemplate, I simply can't entertain in composition.

September 15

Played as much as I could of the opera for Tanya yesterday at Rood's Palazzaccio. I'm sure it was very difficult for her to gain any true impression from my banging and howling. Still her initial comment will always remain my favorite remark about the work, perhaps for sentimental reasons: "What a pity Tony [Sir Tyrone Guthrie, with whom Tanya frequently, and I occasionally, worked] is dead. He would have loved it."

Discography

∾

The Andrée Expedition. Bengt Nordfors, tenor; Bengt Forsberg, piano. Nosag records CD 021.

The Andrée Expedition. William Parker, baritone; William Huckaby, piano. Centaur 2092.

Capriccio for Clarinet and Orchestra (Rossini in Paris). Antony Gigliotti, clarinet; Felix Chiu-sen Chen, conductor, Taipei Symphony. Bravo CD 20125.

Capriccio for Clarinet and Orchestra (Rossini in Paris). Burt Hara, clarinet; Eiji Oue, conductor, Minnesota Orchestra. Reference Recordings RR-100 CD.

Casa Guidi. Frederica von Stade, mezzo; Eiji Oue, conductor, Minnesota Orchestra. Reference Recordings RR-100 CD.

Casanova's Homecoming. Peter Jacoby, music director; Buck Ross, producer and director; Moores Opera Center. Newport Classic NPD85673/2.

Christopher Sly (excerpt). Vern Sutton, tenor; Keith Weber, piano. Ten Thousand Lakes, Schubert Club.

Easter Day. Philip Brunelle, conductor, Ensemble Singers of the Plymouth Music Series. Collins Classics 15232.

Easter Day. Elizabeth C. Patterson, conductor, Gloriæ Dei Cantores. GDCD 008.

From the Diary of Virginia Woolf. Janet Baker, mezzo; Martin Isepp, piano. d'Note Classics DND1019.

From the Diary of Virginia Woolf. Virginia Dupuy, mezzo; Warren Benson, piano. Gasparo GSCD-273.

From the Diary of Virginia Woolf. Mary Ann Hart, mezzo, Dennis Helmrich, piano. Albany Records, Troy 118.

From the Diary of Virginia Woolf. Linn Maxwell, mezzo; William Huckaby, piano. Centaur 2092.

From the Diary of Virginia Woolf. Marta Shèle, mezzo; José Ribera, piano. Proprius 9982.

Gloria (from *The Masque of Angels*). Philip Brunelle, conductor, Plymouth Music Series Chorus and Orchestra. PMS-002.

I Hate and I Love. Rick Kvam, conductor, Choral Arts Ensemble of Rochester et al. CAER-71998.

I Hate and I Love. Robert Shaw, conductor, Robert Shaw Festival Singers et al. Telarc 20 CD-80408.

I Hate and I Love. Dale Warland, conductor, Dale Warland Singers et al. Gothic Records G 49217.

I Hate and I Love. Dale Warland, conductor, Dale Warland Singers et al. Musical Heritage Society MHS 512199Z DDD.

In Praise of Music. Eiji Oue, conductor, Minnesota Orchestra. Reference Recordings RR-100 CD.

Jonah and the Whale. Vern Sutton, tenor; LeRoy Lehr, bass; et al. Philip Brunelle, conductor. PMS-001.

Le Tombeau d'Edgar Poe. Chad Shelton, tenor; Eiji Oue, conductor, Minnesota Orchestra. Reference Recordings RR-91 CD.

Let All the World in Every Corner Sing. Elizabeth C. Patterson, conductor, Gloriæ Dei Cantores. GDCD 010.

Letters from Composers. Patrice Michaels Bedi, soprano; Jeffrey Kust, guitar. Cedille Records CDR 90000 029.

Letters from Composers. Berit Hallqvist, soprano; Mats Bergström, guitar. Fermat FLPD 61.

Letters from Composers. Vern Sutton, tenor; Jeffrey Van, guitar. CRI 291.

Miss Havisham's Wedding Night. Linda Mabbs, soprano; Sara Watkins, conductor, Sinfonia of St. Cecilia. Koch International Classics 3-7388-2 H1.

A Nation of Cowslips. Philip Brunelle, conductor, Ensemble Singers of the Plymouth Music Series. Collins Classics 15232.

Peter Quince at the Clavier. Christopher Riley, piano; Philip Brunelle, conductor, Ensemble Singers of the Plymouth Music Series. Collins Classics 15232.

Peter Quince at the Clavier. Paul Schoenfield, piano; Dale Warland, conductor, Dale Warland Singers. Musical Heritage Society MHS 512199Z DDD.

Postcard from Morocco. Philip Brunelle, conductor, Minnesota Opera. CRI CD 614. Also Desto DC7137 7138.

Reverie, Reflections on a Hymn Tune. Eiji Oue, conductor, Minnesota Orchestra. Reference Recordings RR-91 CD.

A Ring of Time. Eiji Oue, conductor, Minnesota Orchestra. Reference Recordings RR-91 CD.

Royal Invitation. Jorge Mester, conductor, Louisville Orchestra. LS 764.

Royal Invitation. Edward Polochick, conductor, Concert Artists of Baltimore. Sonora S022585 CD.

Six Elizabethan Songs. Patrice Michaels Bedi, soprano; Rembrandt Chamber Players. Cedille Records CDR 90000 011.

Six Elizabethan Songs. Barbara Bonney, soprano; André Previn, piano. London 289 455 511-2.

Six Elizabethan Songs. Jean Danton, soprano; William Moylan, piano. Albany Records, Troy 264.

Six Elizabethan Songs. Melanie Duncan, soprano; Claire Cooper, piano. Move Records MD3212.

Six Elizabethan Songs. Irene Kurka, soprano; Michaela Schlotter, piano. FMMS CD 97-13.

Six Elizabethan Songs. Barbara Martin, soprano; Arthur Weisberg, conductor, baroque ensemble. CRI SD 380.

Six Elizabethan Songs. Frederick Urrey, tenor; Richard Clark, conductor, Manhattan Chamber Players. Newport Classic NPD 85602.

Songs about Spring. Patrice Michaels Bedi, soprano; Elizabeth Buccheri, piano. Cedille Records CDR 90000 029.

Songs about Spring. Jean Danton, soprano; William Moylan, piano. Albany Records, Troy 264.

Spirituals and Swedish Chorales. Philip Brunelle, conductor, Ensemble Singers of the Plymouth Music Series. Collins Classics 15232.

Tango (from *The Dream of Valentino*). David Zinman, conductor, Baltimore Symphony Orchestra. Argo 444 454.

Te Deum (Verba Domini Cum Verbis Populi). Philip Brunelle, conductor, Plymouth Festival Chorus and Orchestra. Virgin Classics VC 59009.

Te Deum (Verba Domini Cum Verbis Populi). Paul Salamunovich, conductor, Los Angeles Master Chorale. RCM12002.

A Thanksgiving to God, for His House. Philip Brunelle, conductor, Ensemble Singers of the Plymouth Music Series. Collins Classics 15232.

To Be Sung upon the Water. Patrice Michaels Bedi, soprano; Elizabeth Buccheri, piano; Larry Combs, clarinet. Cedille Records CDR 90000 029.

To Be Sung upon the Water. John Stewart, tenor; Donald Hassard, piano; Charles Russo, clarinet. Phoenix PHCD 129. Also Desto DC 64443.

To God. Philip Brunelle, conductor, Ensemble Singers of the Plymouth Music Series. Collins Classics 15232.

A Toccata of Galuppi's. Dale Warland, conductor, Dale Warland Singers et al. Gothic Records G 49217.

Valentino Dances. Eiji Oue, conductor, Minnesota Orchestra. Reference Recordings RR-91 CD.

Valse Triste. Eiji Oue, conductor, Minnesota Orchestra. Reference Recordings RR-91 CD.

Variations for Orchestra (The Mask of Night). Maria Jette, soprano; Philip Brunelle, conductor, Plymouth Festival Orchestra. Virgin Classics VC 59009.

Walden Pond. Dale Warland, conductor, Dale Warland Singers et al. Gothic Records G 49217.

A Water Bird Talk. John Shirley-Quirk, baritone; Sara Watkins, conductor, Sinfonia of St. Cecilia. Koch International Classics 3-7388-2 H1.

A Water Bird Talk. Vern Sutton, tenor; Richard Clark, conductor, Manhattan Chamber Orchestra. Newport Classic NPD 85602.

Index

Concerto for Euphonium (Hovhaness), 16

Concerto for Orchestra (Bartók), 166

Concerto Grosso no. 2 for Piano and Strings (Bloch), 9

Conrad, Joseph, xvii, 68

Copland, Aaron, 173

corporate patronage, 28

Corwin, Norman, 19

Cowell, Henry, 6–7, 11, 12, 25, 133

Crashaw, Richard, 155, 156

creative act, xiv–xvii: unforeseen outcomes of, xiv–xv

Cui, César Antonovich, 168

cummings, e e, 1, 10, 105

Cummington School of the Arts (Massachusetts), 1

Curtin, Phyllis, 31, 32

Dale Warland Singers, 110, 170

Dallapiccola, Luigi, 5–6, 10, 11, 12, 72, 122

Dallas Opera, 137, 138, 151–52

Dalrymple, Bernice, 148

Dante Alighieri, 121, 183–85

Davis, Peter G., 29

Debussy, Claude, 168

Dekker, Thomas, 51

Delfs, Andreas, 174

DeLone, Peter, 4, 6, 128

de Musset, Alfred, 11, 121

Denver Lyric Opera, 32–33

Desto Records, 75

detachment from composition: state of, xvi

deWaart, Edo, 71

Diaghilev, Sergei, 2, 68

Dickens, Charles, 91, 92, 101, 107, 164

Dine, Jim, 40

discography, 211–16

Divertimento for Piano and Strings, xvii, 9–12, 21, 143

Divine Comedy (Dante), 184

DiVirgilio, Nicholas, 23, 26, 27

Doctor Faustus (Mann), 49

dodecaphony, 5–6

Donahue, John, 66, 67

Doña Rosita (García Lorca), 10

Don Juan, 20, 21

Doráti, Antal, 27

Downes, Olin, 19

Dream of Valentino, The, 151–54, 171

Dressen, Dan, 151

Duval, Robert, 23

Easter Day, 139–41, 183

Eastman School of Music, 11, 127, 173; compositions written at, 13–25; opera department, coaching, 24–25

eclecticism, 68

Elizabethan Songs, 26–30, 55, 190

Erickson, Raymond, 66

"Erlking" (Schubert), 114

Pancella, Phyllis, 180, 181, 182

Panek, Lorraine, 5

parody: attraction to, 55

Passionate Shepherd, The (Shakespeare), 191

Passion of Jonathan Wade, The (Floyd), 31

Patrick, Julian, 123, 151

Patterson, Elizabeth, 183

Peabody Conservatory, 1–3, 4, 12, 127; music composed at, 2

Pélissier, Olympe, 130

Pennsylvania State University, 104

Perse, Saint-John, 16

Peter Quince at the Clavier, 104–6

Pettersson, Ann-Margaret, 152–53

Phantom Empress, The, 91

Ph.D. thesis, 18

phrasing, 99–100

piano: skill on, 76, 143–44, 160

Piano Concerto (Cowell), 7

Piano Sonata, 2, 144

Picasso, Pablo, 2

Pirandello, Luigi, 5

Plath, Sylvia, 120

Plymouth Congregational Church choir, 73, 95

Plymouth Music Series, 52, 72, 73, 161, 163

Poe, Edgar Allan, 85, 126–27, 143, 196

Polka for Flute and Orchestra, 172

Poné, Gundaris, 108

Pope, Stuart, 30, 58, 70, 84, 91, 118–19

Postcard from Morocco, xviii, 36, 40, 66–68, 162, 163

Prelude for Easter Dawning, 100, 117–19

Prelude in C-Sharp Minor (Rachmaninoff), 168

problem solving, 173

Prokofiev, Sergei, 2, 3

Puccini, Giacomo, 54, 85, 94

Pulitzer Prize, 84

Rachmaninoff, Sergei, 168

Rake's Progress, The (Stravinsky), 2

Rauschenberg, Robert, 40

Ravel, Maurice, 2

Religion: feelings about organized, 156–57

Religious music. *See* choral music

Rendell, Ruth, 171

reputation, making: *Masque of Angels* and, 38; *Postcard from Morocco* and, 66

Rescigno, Nicola, 136

Resurrection of Don Juan, 13–16

Revelation of Saint John the Divine, The, 48–50, 73, 156, 162

Reverie (Debussy), 168

Reverie (Reflections on a Hymn Tune), 177–79

revisions: difficulty of, 61–62; of *Miss Havisham's Fire,* 164–66

∾

Dominick Argento, one of America's leading composers and librettists, has been hailed by *Opera News* and *Time* magazine as the most eminent creator of opera in the United States. He was awarded the Pulitzer Prize in 1975 for the song cycle *From the Diary of Virginia Woolf* and in 2004 received the Grammy for best classical contemporary composition for *Casa Guidi*. From 1958 to 1997 he taught music theory and composition at the University of Minnesota, where he was named Regents' Professor, the university's highest honor.